PSYCHOTHERAPY WITH SEVERELY DEPRIVED CHILDREN

Edited by
Mary Boston and Rolene Szur

Routledge & Kegan Paul
London, Boston, Melbourne and Henley

First published in 1983
by Routledge & Kegan Paul plc
39 Store Street, London WC1E 7DD,
9 Park Street, Boston, Mass. 02108, USA,
296 Beaconsfield Parade, Middle Park,
Melbourne 3206, Australia, and
Broadway House, Newtown Road,
Henley-on-Thames, Oxon RG9 1EN
Printed in Great Britain by
Robert Hartnoll Ltd., Bodmin, Cornwall.

Library of Congress Cataloging in Publication Data

Psychotherapy with severely deprived children.
Bibliography: p.
Includes index.
1. Child psychotherapy - Residential treatment.
2. Child psychotherapy - Residential treatment - England
- London Metropolitan area. I. Boston, Mary.
II. Szur, Rolene. [DNLM: 1. Psychosocial deprivation
- In infancy and childhood - Congresses.
3. Maternal deprivation - In infancy and childhood -
Congresses. 4. Paternal deprivation - In infancy and childhood -
Congresses. WS 105.5.D3 P974]
RJ504.5.P79 1983   618.92'8521   83-3116

ISBN 0-7100-9536-8

To
Esther Bick

who taught us to observe and think about babies and the development of the individual in the ordinary family, inspiring our clinical work and sharpening our appreciation of the deprivation suffered by the children in this book.

CONTENTS

Note: The clinical contributions on the named children in
      Chapters 2, 3, 4, 5, 6, 8, 10 and 11 are published
      anonymously, in the interests of confidentiality. The
      therapists are listed alphabetically with the other
      contributors.

ACKNOWLEDGMENTS

This book owes its being to the many members of a multi-disciplinary workshop which included psychiatrists, social workers, psychologists, educational therapists and child psychotherapists. All have contributed their time, knowledge and experience to thinking about the complex and sometimes distressing issues arising from the work described in these pages. The editors are grateful to Shirley Hoxter who initiated the idea of the workshop and to everyone who contributed, particularly those who provided detailed clinical material, even though it has not been possible for more than a small part of the work to feature in the book. We would like also to thank David Campbell for his contribution on psychological assessment, Shirley Burch who struggled with the data submitted on numerous cases so that some generalisations and comparisons could be attempted and Margaret Hunter for permission to quote some case material. Barbara Forryan has prepared the index with admirable speed.

We appreciate how much we have learned from our patients, a number of whom appear under pseudonyms in these pages. In order to protect the confidentiality of their communications, their therapists are not individually identified and certain incidents and facts have been omitted or disguised, though in a way which we hope preserves the essence of their interactions.

We are extremely indebted to Jane Rayner for her patience in grappling with illegible handwriting in some of the preliminary drafts and to Joyce Piper and Connie Leigh for their meticulous work in preparing the final manuscript.

Finally our thanks are due for the forbearance of our long-suffering families and friends who have had to put up with our preoccupation with editorial duties for a considerable time.

CONTRIBUTORS AND THERAPISTS

Pamela Berse is a child psychotherapist living and working in Kent. Previously she worked at the Tavistock Clinic, the Hospital for Sick Children, Great Ormond Street and the Danbury Hospital, Connecticut. She has been particularly involved in the application of psychoanalytic understanding to paediatric settings.

Mary Boston is a child psychotherapist and senior tutor at the Tavistock Clinic. She worked formerly at the Hospital for Sick Children, Great Ormond Street, where she was particularly interested in work with pre-school children, and has written on current research in child development. She is co-editor with Dilys Daws of 'The Child Psychotherapist and Problems of Young People' (1977).

Ronald S. Britton is a psychoanalyst and consultant psychiatrist in the Department for Children and Parents, Tavistock Clinic, and was formerly consultant to the Social Services Departments of two London boroughs. In connection with his interest in finding means of offering psychotherapeutic help to disturbed families unable to relate to conventional clinic resources, he has been involved in the development of Young Family Centres.

Helen Carr is a psychoanalyst and a child psychotherapist working at Battersea and Slough Child Guidance Units, where in addition to seeing child and adult patients, she also acts in a consultative role to a day nursery and works in a Special Investigation Unit. She has been consultant to a number of children's homes.

Maristella Fontana's contribution is published posthumously. She was a child psychotherapist at Bromley Child Guidance Unit and at the Tavistock Clinic where she participated in teaching. She was also interested in the application of psychoanalytic concepts to education.

Gianna Henry is a child psychotherapist and organising tutor of the Observation Course at the Tavistock Clinic and at Rome University. She works in individual and family therapy in the Adolescent Department at the Tavistock Clinic and has taught on a Tavistock course for staff of residential homes and day nurseries. She took part in a research project into the psychological welfare of young children making long stays in hospital (Dartington et al., 1976).

Eva Holmes is principal educational psychologist in Enfield, and was formerly at the Tavistock Clinic. For some years she was attached to children's homes where she became aware of the special educational needs of deprived children; this led her to set up a pre-school unit for children in day and residential care. She has worked with adoption agencies in placing older or handicapped children.

Shirley Hoxter is a child psychotherapist and senior tutor in the Department for Children and Parents at the Tavistock Clinic. She has engaged in preventive and therapeutic work with deprived or abused children and foster-parents, and has experience of consultative work in a Young Family Day Centre and a children's home. She is co-author of 'Explorations in Autism' (Meltzer et al., 1975).

Joan Hutten is principal social worker in the Department for Children and Parents and co-ordinator for post-qualification trainings for social workers at the Tavistock Clinic. She is consultant to the Thomas Coram Foundation Adoption Project and to two children's homes, and the author of 'Short-term Contracts in Social Work' (1977).

Ann Kaplan was a child psychotherapist at Woodberry Down Child Guidance Unit in East London where she also worked with families. Special interests include consultation to day nurseries and to groups of teachers and other professionals who work with small children. She is currently working in the Department of Psychiatry, University of Chicago.

Gabriella Grauso Malliani is a child psychotherapist at the Cassell Hospital and Richmond Child and Family Psychiatric Clinic and at the Tavistock Clinic where she is also involved in teaching: she formerly worked with patients in some of the paediatric wards at the Hospital for Sick Children, Great Ormond Street.

Lisa Miller is a child psychotherapist and senior tutor at the Tavistock Clinic. She has treated a number of children in care, some on a small group basis, and works in a consultancy capacity with a Young Family Centre and an Assessment Centre.

Sheila Miller is a principal child psychotherapist working at Loughton Child Guidance Clinic, and a senior tutor in the Department for Children and Parents at the Tavistock Clinic. She has been consultant to a children's home for five years and has a special interest in work with children in care.

Michael Morice is a child psychotherapist at the Portman Clinic, working mainly with adolescents, and also at the West London Hospital. Formerly he worked for some years at a day school for maladjusted children in Brixton.

Elizabeth Oliver-Bellasis works as a senior social worker in the

Adolescent Department of the Tavistock Clinic and is also a child psychotherapist. Previously she worked for some years at Northgate Clinic Adolescent In-patient Unit. She is tutor on a part-time course for residential and day care workers.

Elizabeth da Rocha Barros trained as a psychologist in Brazil and at the Sorbonne, and is co-author of several papers on community planning for the welfare of young children. At present she is working as a child psychotherapist at the Child and Family Psychiatric Clinic in Hitchin and at the Tavistock Clinic.

Alan Shuttleworth is a senior social worker employed by the London Borough of Camden in the Department for Children and Parents at the Tavistock Clinic. He is also a child psychotherapist at Kingsbury Child and Family Centre.

Judy Shuttleworth is a child psychotherapist working in the Department of Psychological Medicine at the Hospital for Sick Children, Great Ormond Street. As part of this work she runs a teaching group for the staff of the Department's Day Centre for Young Children and their Families.

Rolene Szur is the principal child psychotherapist at the Hospital for Sick Children, Great Ormond Street, and a senior tutor at the Tavistock Clinic. At the hospital she participates in a family consultation team concerned with problems of child abuse and issues of child care and custody. She has been concerned with the emotional welfare of patients in intensive care units and other paediatric wards.

Brian Truckle is a senior social worker and tutor in social work at the Tavistock Clinic. He trained as a psychiatric social worker and has worked in a variety of statutory and voluntary social agencies. He has written about youth counselling and group work.

Gillian Woodman-Smith worked as a child psychotherapist at Plymouth Nuffield Clinic and also as a supervisor of students on the counselling course at Exeter University. Prior to this she worked at the Tavistock Clinic and is now working at the Marlborough Day Hospital.

INTRODUCTION

This book draws on the experience of some eighty severely deprived children referred for individual psychoanalytic psychotherapy to the Tavistock and other clinics and schools in the London area.

All these patients were in community care at the time of treatment, most living in children's homes and a few in foster-care. They came from chaotic and disrupted families, nearly half from unsupported parents who had been unable to cope. Many of the children had experienced abuse and neglect.

Children from such backgrounds have often not been considered suitable for psychotherapy both because of the practical difficulties and because they may be thought to be too emotionally damaged to make use of it.

Research studies have shown that there is without doubt a continuing high rate of emotional and behavioural disturbance among children in community care. Despite the hope currently being invested in the provision of foster-placements and adoption, this remains a vulnerable group, who may grow up to perpetuate the cycle of deprivation, becoming the inadequate or abusing parents of another generation of disturbed children.

A report published in the UK by the Social Science Research Council (1980) calls for research into the needs of children in care - for 'fine meshed descriptive studies' which might help us to learn something of 'the experience and the quality of life of these children'. Such studies might hopefully lead to provision which would enable young people to leave care 'emotionally and intellectually strengthened rather than more difficult and damaged than when they entered it'.

Psychoanalytical psychotherapy is one kind of treatment which aims at the emotional and intellectual strengthening suggested. It aims to explore in depth the child patient's feelings and experience at both conscious and unconscious levels. As psychotherapy is a relatively long-term treatment it does afford an opportunity for long-term study of some children which in many cases illuminates the vicissitudes of their lives.

Chapter 1 describes how child psychotherapists found themselves treating an increasing number of severely deprived children and how a multi-disciplinary workshop was set up to study and review the experience gained.

Subsequent chapters give some illustrative material from the work with some of the patients, together with discussions of related theoretical and technical issues. Later chapters illustrate the support and contributions necessary from other members of the multi-disciplinary team.

The authors hope that by sharing their experience of the inner worlds of some of these children, they may make a contribution, albeit small, to the study of the needs of deprived children.

The experiences of the therapists struggling, often painfully, to establish contact and communication with young people who have been hurt and disillusioned by life, provides in many cases illuminating material on the children's perceptions of their interrelationships which may be of relevance to all who are in close contact with such children.

Chapters 7, 13 and 14 in particular explore the ways in which it is hoped the book may be of use to others working with deprived children in different contexts. In Chapter 15 some attention is given to the strong feelings which may be aroused in all who work in this field.

We hope that this material can afford us a deeper understanding of the different kinds of reactions to deprivation. This may help us to provide more adequately for the needs, not only of those children who have the opportunity to receive psychotherapy, but of many others.

1 THE TAVISTOCK WORKSHOP: AN OVERALL VIEW

Mary Boston

Emotional deprivation is hard to define and can occur in many contexts including the ordinary intact family, where there may be an area of experience which the child has felt as deprivation (Winnicott, 1966). When there has been actual lack, disruption or distortion of basic parental care, as with the children we are writing about, the effect of such experiences on their personality development becomes a question of concern.

Research studies indicate that discontinuity of emotional care in the early years may have serious effects on a child's capacity to establish trusting and secure relationships as well as on the ability to think and to learn (e.g. Bowlby, 1951; Ainsworth, 1962; Britton, 1978; Holmes, 1980). Other studies have suggested that recovery from the damaging effects of adverse early experience may be possible if circumstances later become more favourable (Clarke and Clarke, 1979). However, the early stress and rejection from families in turmoil are, sadly, usually continuing (Wolkind and Rutter, 1973).

The still high rate of foster breakdown (Wolkind, 1978) leaves us no room for complacency, although recent evidence by Tizard (1977) that adoption after babyhood may be more successful than fostering because of the greater security it engenders is encouraging.

Psychotherapy with deprived children, however, has often been considered difficult or inadvisable. Brill and Thomas (1965) found that once weekly treatment may not be sufficient. Winnicott (1965), in writing about therapy with the deprived child, warned of the dangers of acting out and the need in some cases for residential placement. Dockar-Drysdale (1968) considered the provision of 'primary emotional experience' in a residential setting to be essential for some children before interpretative psychotherapy is possible.

Alternative ways of helping have been developed by many child guidance clinics, including the Tavistock Department for Children and Parents. Consultation and support is offered to field and residential social workers and there has been work with foster- and adoptive parents (see Chapter 13). Paradoxically, it has been this supportive work, rather than theoretical considerations, which has led to further attempts to engage deprived children in psychotherapy.

Bobby
Such was the case with Bobby whose psychotherapy was described in earlier publications (Boston, 1967 and 1972). The housemother, in the course of discussions with the local clinic's psychiatrist, com-

plained that 6½-year-old Bobby was the most difficult child to manage in the home. He showed violent emotional responses, was demanding, verbally obscene and abusive, showing some delinquent tendencies. But it was his suicidal threats and asthma attacks which really alarmed the staff. It seemed urgent to see if some help could be offered to this particular child and to the staff of his home, and in spite of considerable practical difficulties, psychotherapy was embarked on, at first weekly and subsequently more frequently. Bobby had been in care since before his second birthday, and had been in and out of care and hospital before that. He was in a residential nursery until he was 5.

Looking back on this case in the light of the subsequent experience of the workshop cases, I think it may well have been some quality in the child which singled him out for such special treatment. Although so difficult, he was liked by those who cared for him. He made a good initial contact in treatment and retained hopefulness in spite of his unfortunate experiences. At the beginning he eagerly sought help, confiding in the therapist, telling her of his loneliness. He showed a pattern of behaviour which was subsequently observed in other deprived patients, an initial 'honeymoon' period of idealised contact followed by abrupt disillusionment at the first inevitable frustration. This kind of behaviour is of course very familiar to the staff of children's homes. It was his swings of mood which made Bobby so difficult to cope with. The controlling blackmailing behaviour he used to defend himself against the painfulness of a dependent relationship made it hard for the staff to offer the necessary substitute mothering.

It was hard too for the therapist, for although her task was different, she inevitably encountered similar problems, and, as therapy proceeded she received the full force of his acute resentment and hate against parental figures experienced as cruelly abandoning.

The therapist's capacity to endure and 'contain' the confused turmoil of resentful and hostile feelings which Bobby conveyed by means of physical actions was tested to the full and, because of his violence, it was sometimes touch and go whether therapy could continue. However it seemed most important that the therapist should survive and show some strength, in contrast to the fragile figures of Bobby's inner world and past experience. After a year of very difficult and arduous work, Bobby began to gain more control over his violent outbursts and some reconstruction of his internal world and development of more trusting and concerned relationships could proceed. He began to spare the therapist some of the messiness and attacks, and even said 'thank you' after a session. He began to show an appreciation of the community's concern for him in the shape of city maps with civic amenities prominently featuring. The 'chip on the shoulder' of being a second-class citizen, a 'black bastard' (his own words), was gradually showing some signs of giving way to a better self-image. His behaviour in the children's home improved dramatically. He was no longer the most difficult child. The housemother was, however, concerned that he seemed depressed.

Bobby's treatment took several years, an expensive investment in time and commitment for all concerned. The outcome, however, seemed hopeful. Perhaps, although not easily reversible, the damaging effects of early deprivation might be alleviated by appropriate therapy. If this could be done and follow up could confirm its long-term value, then the cost might be considerably less than expenditure on institutional management which might have been necessary at a later stage of his life.

Martin
A further account of psychotherapy with a deprived child was pub-lished by Henry (1974) in her paper, Doubly Deprived. Again a West Indian boy who had made a suicidal attempt and who alarmed all in his environment, this 14-year-old, in contrast to Bobby, had had a long period in foster-care, although he had also had an early period of deprivation. The foster-care had however broken down because of his increasingly unmanageable behaviour and he was living in a children's home at the time of treatment. Martin was also unlike Bobby in that he did not show such initial confidingness in therapy. He had a numb, unreachable quality which the therapist found very hard to get through. In Martin's words to her, she was 'talking to a brick wall'. This brick-wall quality was very hard to penetrate and, although expressed differently, had a quality of forceful projection of unpleasant and painful feelings into the therapist that was similar to that of Bobby's violent behaviour. With Martin there was a menacing quality, with a continual threat of violence, suggested by the wearing of knuckle rings, the produc-tion of knives and remarks such as, 'We'll have to get a new Mrs Henry.' Again the need seemed to be protection from painful feel-ings of dependence. 'You can get your face wet with rain, with tears, with blood and yours is going to be wet with blood before mine is wet with tears.'

Henry described this hard, brick-wall defensive, thick-skinned attitude as leading to a double deprivation. Martin suffered not only the deprivation inflicted on him by external circumstances but he deprived himself further by his crippling defences which made him so hard to get in touch with. The essence of this 'double deprivation', which has been observed to some degree in all the children in care in psychotherapy, is the identification with an un-feeling, cruel, abandoning parental figure. This figure in the child's inner world tends to be perceived in other people. Thus the child might experience the therapist (as indeed other would-be helpers) as cold and unfeeling and even cruel. As Martin's hardness dim-inished he accused Mrs Henry of being herself a cold person coming from a cold country and her central heating was described as 'cold water running through a mass of metal'. It makes a great deal more sense of much of the seemingly unreasonable or outrageous behaviour of many deprived children if one bears in mind that they are often doing to others what they experience as being done to them, both externally and internally.

Another aspect of Martin's deprivation which is highlighted by

Henry in her paper is the impairment of the capacity to think. She
develops this theme further in Chapter 9. (See also Chapter 8).
Most of the deprived children studied have considerable learning
difficulties. These are discussed in Chapter 7.

With Martin, as with Bobby, a considerable amount of patient and
arduous work did seem to produce a shift to a more thoughtful and
concerned attitude in which at times at least he could acknowledge
greater trust in the therapist and greater awareness of his need for
help. He no longer gave cause for concern either at school or at the
home.

These published cases of psychotherapy with severely deprived
children suggested the possibility of a hopeful outcome, in spite
of the difficulties experienced in the course of therapy.

THE WORKSHOP

Meanwhile, Tavistock staff in consultations with social workers and
residential staff found themselves at times under pressures similar
to those experienced by Bobby's psychiatrist - 'to do something
about a particular child'. In other cases, in order to be able to
offer appropriate advice on placement, it seemed essential to get to
know the child in some depth. Sometimes a small group of children
was seen regularly by a child psychotherapist for a period, with a
view to assessing the specific needs of the children. It became clear
that many of these children were able to make use of a therapeutic
relationship and a gradually increasing number of them, living in
children's homes or in foster-care, have in recent years come into
psychotherapy. A workshop was convened in order to study and
review the experience gained.

At the time of writing information was available on some features
of the psychotherapy of eighty severely deprived children, all in
community care, and in current or fairly recent psychotherapy in
the Department for Children and Parents or at other clinics. Some
of these will later be described in detail. Attendance has varied
from once to five times per week, half coming once weekly. Most
have attended for a year or more (a few much longer), quite a
proportion being still in ongoing treatment. In nine cases, the
therapy was known to have been broken off prematurely in the view
of the therapist, either by the child or for external reasons. The
age range of the children was 4 to 18 years on starting therapy.

We do not know how representative of children in care these
patients are. They may constitute a highly selected sample. It
may be that there was something about these particular children
that made them more likely to be referred for help. The reasons
given for referral were very varied but in many cases were to do
with the pain and anxiety they evoked in others. Sometimes the
behaviour complained of was alarming, as with Bobby and Martin,
or unbearable as with Eileen; sometimes it was appealing; sometimes
there had been traumatic experiences, as with Lesley. Very often
the children were likeable, even if difficult, and thought to be

capable of getting in touch with their feelings. It could be argued
that they unconsciously sought help and that this was a hopeful
sign. In half the cases the referral arose out of the consultation
work mentioned.

The sample was selected on the basis that the therapists were able
either to present detailed descriptions to the workshop or to submit
relevant data on their cases, irrespective of the success or otherwise of the venture. Many of the patients were still in therapy so
the outcome is as yet unknown, but usually an improvement in the
child's behaviour outside the treatment in the home setting and at
school was reported, even in those cases where therapy had been
broken off prematurely.

Some consideration was given in the workshop to those children
in care referred but who were not recommended for individual
psychotherapy. A systematic comparison of this group of children
with the 'psychotherapy group' was not possible, largely because
the data about the former group seemed inadequate for a fair
comparison. The situation was further complicated by the fact that
the hopefulness aroused by the progress of some of the earlier
cases had led to a gradual change in policy in the department
regarding the offering of psychotherapy to deprived children. A
preliminary look at some of the Tavistock cases suggested that by
the time the study was undertaken, failure to get into therapy was
more likely to be due to lack of support in the external environment than to differences in the types of problems presented or in
the personalities of the children. The fact that in many cases,
where there had been some initial assessment, subsequent appointments were failed so that there was no one to whom any recommen-
dations could be made illustrates the point made by Britton (Chapter
12) that 'psychotherapy needs a viable, comprehensible and predictable framework in which it can take place.'

In general we have found that for therapy to be successfully
established a great deal of support is required from the very
many people involved in the children's day-to-day care. The help
of colleagues in maintaining liaison with the caring network has
been indispensable to the psychotherapists (Hutten, 1977; Britton,
1977). Such support, which has been a crucial factor in maintaining the children in therapy, is described more fully in Chapter 13.

TREATMENT APPROACH

The psychotherapists were all trained at the Tavistock Clinic and
followed a similar method of treatment based on Melanie Klein's
(1932, p. 29) view that 'The child expresses its phantasies, its
wishes and its actual experiences in a symbolic way through play
and games.' An important aspect of this kind of therapy is the
offering of a predictable and regular time and place for the sessions, a time which is exclusively for the patient and protected, as
far as humanly possible, from interruptions and intrusion. This
is a time in which the therapist can give sole attention to the child,

'a space in the mind', as described by Shirley Hoxter in her paper on Play and Communication (1977, p. 210). It may be a unique experience for many children, and especially for deprived children, to have an adult's receptive attention in this way. A small box of toys is provided for the use of each child, toys which lend themselves to imaginative play, such as small animals and human figures, drawing materials and plasticine. Although some children never use them, they do assist some patients, particularly younger ones, to communicate their feelings and thoughts to the therapist. The therapist maintains a neutral, non-directive attitude, within the confines of the time and space allocated, and does not offer reassurance in the form of food or gifts. An attempt is made to understand with the child his communications, both conscious and unconscious, whether by play, words or non-verbal means, and to express this understanding in simple words - 'interpretations'. This is part of the process of helping the patient to gain insight into his behaviour by means of his experience in the session with the therapist. The way this developing 'transference' relationship between therapist and patient illuminates and also modifies the child's characteristic ways of relating to other important figures in his life will become clearer in subsequent chapters.

ASSESSMENT FOR PSYCHOTHERAPY

It has already been indicated that most of these children came into therapy for reasons which were more to do with their external situation and the potential for support in their environment than with any precise assessment of their suitability for this kind of treatment. If we follow Winnicott (1965) in recognising that much of their anti-social and problem behaviour is in fact a plea for help and consider that these particular children were indeed asking for it, we have to face the fact that many other children in similar situations may make such pleas which are unheard or cannot be responded to. Often a decision was made on the basis of the therapist's estimate of his or her ability to get in touch with the child, perhaps on the basis of 'Let's try and see.'

Some of the children had a psychological assessment. An educational psychologist discusses some of the characteristic patterns shown in the tests in Chapter 7.

Historical factors have often been thought to be relevant in predicting response to therapy; the more severe the history of deprivation the less hopeful it is thought to be that the child can make use of the therapeutic relationship. We have tried to examine this hypothesis in looking at the histories of the patients discussed in the workshop. Unfortunately, information about the early histories of the children is often very sketchy. Possibly this is characteristic of children in care.

Even when pretty detailed factual histories are available it is usually not possible to know the quality of the care received in the first few months of life. Britton (1978, p. 376) points out that the

history, however carefully taken, 'may not do sufficient justice to
some of the details of early infantile care.' Recent research on
infants suggests the importance of a synchronous interaction
developing between mother and baby from the time of birth, or
perhaps before, an interaction which determines subsequent
interactions and which needs continuity for satisfactory development (Brazelton *et al.*, 1975). The disruptions in such continuity
experienced by the children in our sample can mostly only be
speculated on or deduced from the quality of behaviour during the
course of the psychotherapy itself. Even in those cases where
infancy was spent in residential care, where considerable disruption of continuity of interaction seems inevitable, we do not know
precisely how much mothering and personalised care the children
received.

Most of the eighty children studied, however, have been severely
deprived of parental care, nearly half having been born into
single-parent families. In thirty-four cases the mother was chron-
ically ill or dead, and nineteen children had no current contact
with either parent. A third had experienced foster breakdown,
some having had several placements. The majority were living in
children's homes at the time of referral but seventeen were in
foster-care (see Table 1.1). Over half experienced the final break
from the natural family before the age of 4, some considerably
earlier, and twenty-five had suffered physical abuse or neglect.

An interesting and possibly significant finding is that although
we are in general only too painfully aware that there is often a lack
of continuity of care due to changes of staff and placements, these
particular children have, in spite of their deprivation in infancy,
apparently all experienced some period of stable care at some later
stage in their lives. This might be in the same children's home or
with the same house- or foster-mother, though further examination of staff change affecting individual children would be required
to substantiate this impression. The relevance of even some period
of stable care to their capacity to use a therapeutic relationship
might well be worth exploring further, and would be in line with
research work by Mia Kellmer Pringle (1974) and Wolkind (1977a).
They report that a lasting relationship with an adult makes a significant difference to the adjustment of children in long-term
institutional care.

Table 1.1 Children in care in psychotherapy

	Children's homes*	Foster-care*	Own home*	Total
Boys	36	8	0	44
Girls	26	9	1	36
Total	62	17	1	80

*At start of psychotherapy.

While it was certainly not true in this sample that a history of
severe deprivation was a contra-indication to being able to make contact with the therapist, it proved difficult to make generalisations
about the relationship between the severity of the deprivation and
the use made of psychotherapy.

However it is suggestive that some children who spent their
earliest weeks in incubators in hospital and were also deprived of
early mothering and even physical holding seemed to show effects
of their early experience in the flat two-dimensional kind of personalities they have developed. These children, mostly girls, unheld
in infancy, seem to lack any kind of boundary or containing function themselves. Some of them will be described more fully in
Chapter 3. It was also true that some children who aroused a good
deal of concern about their future did in fact have histories of
very severe and early deprivation (e.g. Keith, Leroy, Eileen).

GENERAL TRENDS

How have these eighty children fared in psychotherapy? What have
we learnt? Can we draw any conclusions from our experiences to
date? Has it been a fruitful and worthwhile exercise?

It is not easy to generalise because each child in this largish
group emerges as a unique individual, who has developed his or
her own way of coping with the deprivation experienced. Yet
there are some strikingly similar themes.

I think we could say that these deprived children are by no
means easy to treat. Many of them present considerable technical
problems in the management of therapy. Treatment can be an arduous task for patient and therapist alike.

The most illuminating aspect of this study has been the vivid and
dramatic way in which all the children have managed to convey to
their therapists the intensely painful emotional experiences they
have suffered, in spite of their individually different ways of communicating.

Characteristic has been the lack of expectation of any continuity
- much more marked than with the ordinary child in therapy. 'Will
I be seeing you till the next lady comes?', 'Will I be passed on to
someone else?', are typical questions. After a missed session, an
adolescent girl in care explained that she had not bothered to let
the therapist know because she thought it was like the dentist –
they wouldn't notice if you didn't come. The idea of an adult's
continued concern and attention is foreign to many of them.
Regular attendance can therefore be harder to establish and breaks
can be more disruptive, repeating the numerous separation traumas
already experienced. Anxiety about not having enough time comes
up frequently in remarks such as 'How long have I got?' and
references to thousands of years. This is one of the sources of
pain – how can a limited amount of therapy ever be enough for
children who have been deprived of permanent parents?

A strikingly frequent theme in the play of many of the children

is falling - either toys are dropped or the patient himself perches
or jumps or falls perilously. There seems to be a concrete enactment of having been dropped or got rid of. One could see this kind
of behaviour as expressing a feeling of being unheld by a caring
person. The feeling of having been discarded is quite often expressed by the child's looking scruffy, uncared for or by his actual
soiling.

Many sessions can be described as endless evacuation into the
therapists of chaotic, confused and unwanted feelings. This process
may be expressed by a stream of talk or abuse or by actually throwing things and attacking the therapist. Silence, too, can be experienced as a 'perpetual silent scream', in the words of one therapist.
As Keith (Chapter 4) described it, 'the session is a never ending
poo.' These children, as the residential staff well know, take a lot
of putting up with. However, it is perhaps precisely the capacity
of nearly all these patients to use the opportunity which the
therapy offers for some expression and understanding of these unacceptable feelings that leads to the beginnings of some feeling of
hopefulness and of trust in being more cared for. Despair, in the
words of Keith's therapist, both for the patient and therapist,
seems to be related to a sense of there being 'no one and no way
for experiences to be caught and held'. An important function of
the therapist seems to have been to experience and to bear, and
gradually to reflect on, intolerable anxieties on behalf of the
patients. It is only after a considerable period of time that the
patients are able to take back some of these feelings and to begin
to come to terms with them. Following the thinking of Wilfred Bion
(1962) we could see this function of the therapist as being like
that of a mother who can be receptive to the anxieties communicated
to her by her infant, 'the nameless dreads', and by her understanding 'reverie' and response, can make these unthinkable
anxieties more meaningful and bearable to the baby. This important
mental function of the mother Bion calls 'containing', and it is in
this sense that the word 'contain' is used in this book. It is akin to
Donald Winnicott's (1965) term 'holding', not only in the arms but
in the mind and attention and to the 'space in the mind' described
by Hoxter (1977) (see also Chapter 9).

Most of the patients have probably been deprived of much experience of this sort of containment in infancy. Bion (1959, pp. 102-5)
suggests that the poignancy of the deprivation may be rendered
more acute when the patient is allowed an opportunity of which he
has hitherto been cheated. This may account for the forcefulness
of the projections of many of these children. It is an apparent
paradox that this increasing awareness of what they may have
missed is often felt by many of the children to be a very painful,
even torturing experience. There is sometimes the feeling that this
pain is being deliberately inflicted by the therapist, as long-
forgotten feelings are stirred up. Many of the patients try to deal
with these intolerable feelings by reversing the situation and inflict-
ing pain on the therapists instead, thereby hoping to alleviate their
own (see Chapters 6 and 15).

It is hardly surprising, in view of the fact that nearly half the sample had unsupported mothers, that there is an absence of much concept of a firm protective father in the material of these patients. The unknown father tends in phantasy to be a destructive figure with whom the boys are often unconsciously identified. In some cases there was the conviction of growing up to become a criminal. Much of the aggressive behaviour seen in therapy can be understood as taking place under the domination of phantasies of being in the shoes of very bad or cruel figures, e.g. a mother who abandons, or a sadistic father.

The other side of this picture may be a marked idealisation of parental figures. Many deprived children show terrific family loyalty and touchiness on the subject. Such idealisation may remain very cut off from the child's actual experiences and constitute a very defended area kept apart from the therapist. This idealisation matches in intensity the extremely bad parental images inevitably there. The pain of bringing these two aspects of experience together into a more realistic conception of the parents is intense. Sometimes the bad parental image is projected on to the therapist with a consequent threat to the continuation of the therapy. When such a splitting process goes on in the residential setting, as with Chris (see Chapter 3) it can make the children very hard to manage. It is also hard for foster-parents who are attempting to substitute for such idealised parents. A vivid example of a foster-child's extreme idealisation of his own mother is given in Chapter 11.

The ethical problems involved in the exposure of such hurt children to more pain, by attempting to modify their defences, inevitably touching raw spots, has been a matter for concern in the workshop. The sequestering and limiting of this painful process as far as possible to the consulting room, apart from the child's ordinary life, is probably necessary both for the child and the residential staff. A space where hostile and negative feelings in particular can be contained and understood does help to free the child from the compulsion to repeat the past. Then, he can often, outside the therapy, respond more positively to those who are attempting to offer him substitute care and parenting. The psychotherapist's task is not to attempt to give such parenting nor to attempt to right wrongs of the past, but to help the patient to be able to respond to the help and affection of those who are offering parental care.

These child patients show a good deal in common in their reactions to therapy and in the steady progress which most of them can make, provided the therapist can stick it out in the difficult phases. However there are differences in the kinds of initial contact made and in the types of personality pattern which particular children have developed. No single picture of 'the' deprived child emerges. The ensuing chapters describe the struggles of a variety of different children to come to terms, in their own particular ways, with the circumstances of their lives.

2   FALLING AND BEING DROPPED

Lesley
When Lesley was 4 years old her mother died suddenly and in very tragic circumstances.

Like so many of the children in our group of patients she had never known her father. During her early years she had often been taken into a children's home when her young mother felt unable to meet the needs of a small baby, coming herself from a family where members had been in and out of care at various periods. There was also suspicion of physical abuse from a man who was living with them. After her mother's death Lesley was placed with foster-parents but this broke down, partly at least because of her own difficult behaviour, and it was not long before she was returned to the children's home. There the staff felt very concerned about her because of her tragic experiences and also because of a certain cold, 'unnatural' quality in her relationships. The school and educational psychologist noted her 'too good' and excessively self-reliant and controlled behaviour. Following consultation and psychological assessment (see chapter 7), she was referred for psychotherapy with the hope that this would help her to come to terms with her experiences and eventually enable her to be successfully fostered.

All who are professionally concerned with children whose early lives have been so disrupted stress the importance of providing continuity and constancy of relationships for them, and deprecate the many changes of staff which disturb their lives in institutional care. Lesley was a little more fortunate in this respect since she was placed in the same children's home which had received her into care for periods as a baby, and was able to have some experience of continuity with the same housemother, if not with those who cared for her from day to day. Unfortunately we ourselves were unable in Lesley's case to maintain the standard of continuity which we regard as very important, and it became necessary for her to change from one therapist to another during the course of therapy. One can see in the material which follows that this adds to her insecurity and leads to some temporary loss of development. It also shows the way in which such changes of significant figures in her life reactivate feelings about the death of her mother, and it proves possible for these to be helpfully integrated through working within the therapeutic relationship.

In going through these experiences and re-experiences with Lesley the therapists are able to link them together and help her to

11

be more in touch with her sense of loss, to find new and more hopeful ways of responding to it. They do not offer a replacement for the lost mother, nor a representative in the outer world of an early ideal image of a mother. What they do offer is the opportunity for a relationship through which Lesley can explore, experience and find her own feelings about her 'internal objects' or images. By clarifying for the child the nature of her current experiences in terms of the transference relationship to her therapists, by consistency in this and in preparing her for the experience of changes, a new sense of continuity in her inner world begins to come to life, and helps her to feel more confidence in the supportive figures in her external world.

Lesley's first therapist gives us a picture of the little girl when she came into therapy a month or so before her sixth birthday. Before commencing treatment the therapist had met the staff concerned at the children's home, and also Lesley's aunt and social worker.

Part I: The beginning of therapy She was a slim, rather waif-like child, with a slight air of bravado in her quite uninhibited, too easy and undiscriminating way of relating to someone who was, in fact, a complete stranger.

In her first session Lesley tried to skip, unsuccessfully, with a length of string, then quickly demanded that a skipping rope should be provided for her. Such demands for material things proved to be characteristic of her early days in treatment, perhaps as a substitute for what she most deeply lacked.

The other thing which stands out in recalling her early weeks in treatment was the far from waif-like manner in which she used her body. It was as if she could most clearly experience a sense of self through physical activity. One is reminded of Freud's (1923, p. 26) statement that 'the ego is first and foremost a bodily ego.' Lesley was in fact very wiry and agile and spent much of the time trying to master handstands and other acrobatic feats against the wall or on cushions from the couch, falling many times in the process and turning herself and her world upside down. She was demonstrating, I felt, in a very graphic way, through the most primitive means available to her - her body - an aspect of her experience of the world, of her infancy and of her early years. It was possible to help her to understand how these activities might express repetitions of her feelings of being let down, dropped or allowed to fall. Similarly when she asked to have her feet held lest she should literally fall, this seemed a reflection of her need for someone to hold some intolerable feelings of insecurity, painful loss and sadness, and also rage, envy and greed, until such time as she would be able to face them herself without fear of being destroyed by them.

There were other moments when her acrobatic feats appeared provocative and were sometimes accompanied by sexually suggestive rhymes. Her precocious and excessive interest in sexual matters was arousing a great deal of anxiety in the staff at the children's

home and it was this behaviour, as well as the mother's death and
the failed foster-placement, which led the psychiatrist who consulted
to the home to refer her for treatment. The psychiatrist felt that
without psychotherapeutic help, Lesley could, in adolescence,
become delinquent in a promiscuous way and hoped that long-term
help might prevent such an eventuality. Chris, described in the
next chapter, illustrates vividly the anxieties aroused by sexually
provocative behaviour in adolescents. It was realised that Lesley
had in all probability been exposed to her mother's sexual experiences. The emotionally damaging aspects of such exposure are
discussed in Chapter 5.

Lesley's anxieties about being dropped or abandoned were soon
revealed at the first holiday break in treatment. The therapist was
now felt to be the abandoning one. Lesley responded with a seemingly flippant 'who cares', but found it difficult to allow her
therapist to explore this with her. She seemed to fear that nobody
cared enough to stay with her, to keep her, and evidently wondered
whether her demands drove people away. Gradually she became
more able to hear about the coming separation, and to think about
her fears that the therapist might not return. Time began to take
on a new dimension for her.

When the therapist linked her going away on leave with Lesley's
experience of losing her mother and spoke about Lesley's attempt
to keep painful feelings at bay, the child answered, 'Anyway I
can't be sad, can I? Because I'm always smiling,' but went on to
show her desperate need to belong and have someone to cling to.
She said, 'Anyway, she's still my mummy isn't she? Even if she's
dead,' and, 'I'm lucky, at least I've got a daddy.' Later on in
treatment it was possible through rhymes she chanted as she
bounced a ball to talk more meaningfully with her about her search
for her true identity. Who was she? Who was her daddy? What was
his surname? Why had he left them? She showed her fear that it was
her fault and her constant search for him and for her mother in
everyone she saw as she repeatedly sang certain songs.

> On the hill there stands a lady
> Who she is I cannot tell
> All she wants is gold and silver
> All she wants is a fine young man.

Another song suggested her difficulty in becoming aware of her
sadness because of its pain, while the therapist found the pain and
her denial of it at moments as difficult to bear as her foster-parents
had done. She sang 'Poor Jenny stood a-weepin' on a bright
summer's day'. Lesley's mother died in mid-summer.

When the children in her home made cards for Mother's Day Lesley
was reported to have made one too, announcing 'My mummy's dead'
and throwing the card up in the air so it could 'go to mummy in
the sky'. (Her aunt had told her that the two brightest stars in
the sky were her mummy's eyes.)

By the time Lesley was needing to face transfer to a new therapist, she had made considerable progress in getting in touch with some of her feelings and consequently felt a much more 'real' little girl. She still fought against acknowledging her need of others but made less omnipotent claims about being able to do it all herself. Both the staff of the home and the aunt reported that she could now 'dare to be naughty' in a more childlike way. However Lesley was attempting to deal with yet another loss of a significant person in her life in the way which had probably contributed to the breakdown of her foster-placement, that is by splitting processes, as described in Chapter 1. The new therapist was idealised as a bountiful, all-providing figure while the departing therapist seemed to turn, in her mind, to a hostile, damaged and dying figure who was abandoning her. A phantasy appeared in her drawings and play of someone like the therapist being eaten alive by ants, and seemed to express an unconscious wish to punish her for subjecting Lesley to a further loss. At other times, however, she was able to face briefly something of the pain of separation, with less denial and therefore more hope of preserving some memory of a good experience.

In the next illustration, by the second therapist, we see a Lesley who is more than two years older. Again she shows a fluctuation between defensive shutting out behaviour and glimpses - perhaps more frequent now - of vulnerable feelings. This time it is the new therapist's turn to feel shut out, while Lesley plays endlessly with the balls given by her previous worker. The change seems to have led, in the first term, to a temporary setback, a denial of the need for help and some retreat from the beginnings of being in touch which had grown over the previous period. The change itself and the further holiday breaks present new demands for working through the many conflicting feelings about separation and loss. This account focuses on the development of these feelings, which within the structure of the psychotherapeutic setting are most clearly evidenced in relation to breaks. The material highlights the patient work over a period of time, which is necessary for such emotional scars to be healed and for a healthy mourning process to be accomplished. Feelings and phantasies about her mother's death and her absent father have to be reworked through, again and again.
    The period of therapy to be described covers an Easter break and a reorganisation in the home as well as the approach of Christmas. Play material and pictures dramatically express some of her deepest feelings about loss and death and convey the beginning of hope and forgiveness.

Part 2:   The continuation of therapy   When I first met her, Lesley was an attractive girl of 8 with a bright, perky air and slightly pointed face, though at other times when she came to therapy one could still glimpse a little waif. There was an appealing quality about her. In approach she was quite a show man but somehow this never completely masked an underlying appeal and fragility. Often it was as if she had to put on a show in order to be quite sure that my attention was engaged.

Characteristically Lesley would appear to be engrossed in a comic when I went to the waiting room, and there was always a marked hesitation before looking up, as if to say, 'I'll come in my time, I'm doing something and you've interrupted it - you can wait.'
Usually she came to the clinic with a member of staff from the children's home who sometimes waited or went out shopping to return in time for the end of the session. Sometimes other children from the home came with her, and Lesley's attitude to them was one of 'this is my place' as she told them what they could and could not do. Any curiosity that they showed was put down and she left the waiting room with a flaunt and 'see you when I come back.'

If, however, there did happen to be any difficulty over transport or escort Lesley became extremely anxious. On one such occasion when she had been looking out of the window waiting for the car, she suddenly became very angry and upset: 'Bet they'll be late, the other time I waited for ages and they didn't come.' Then her voice became more panicky: 'I'm sure they'll forget and they'll leave me here all night. . . .' It is important to stress that the children's home staff were in fact consistent and regular in ensuring that Lesley had an escort to her sessions, often when this was difficult for them, and over a number of years. But to Lesley the slightest indication that she might be forgotten triggered off anxieties that she was forgotten for ever.

Throughout her treatment Lesley's contact with me fluctuated as she struggled internally with two very different aspects of herself which characteristically alternated rapidly within the same session. There was the part that fought very hard against any dependency needs and used various defensive manoeuvres to achieve this goal. This aspect came across in the manner and flavour of her communications rather than in the content of the material in the sessions. The other part was infinitely more needy and vulnerable. I have called this the infant part, which once open to its needs was liable to experience intense pain, glimpses of which she sometimes trusted me to share. It was often very hard to hold on to this side of herself, for the moment she felt in contact with her vulnerability Lesley had to deny and dismiss her needs, or sometimes to convert them into a certain sexual excitement, in this way repeating features which had begun to be explored during her first period of treatment.

The predominant themes during Lesley's first term with me were her contempt and dismissiveness, and her statement in so many ways of 'I don't need you, I can manage on my own.' She played often with two balls which had been retained from her previous therapy. One ball had been stripped of its outer covering when Lesley had learnt that her first therapist was leaving. The balls were usually used together in very adept juggling games between them, the wall and herself, while keeping me excluded. These games, seemingly endless, were accompanied by a whole variety of songs. Sometimes I was allowed to take up their meaning but at other times the songs would drown me out, and if I found a space to speak she would soon resume the singing. There was a brittle one-upmanship in her manner, replying to enquiries with 'Don't you know, silly', or simply seeming not to hear when I spoke. She could be incredibly irritating or condescending and at its most potent this had a quite devastating effect on my efforts to keep my attention and maintain an interest. She seemed to be projecting pain and anger, but also exposing the hostile indifference which might follow. It was as if this was the most vivid and powerful way Lesley had of conveying to me just how she herself felt about being left by her previous therapist, or by me at the end of every session. She also conveyed that these experiences in the present carried feelings and memories of past separations and in particular some aspects of the loss of her mother. She made me know in myself what it felt like to be excluded, discarded and shut out. Suddenly I would find myself experiencing extraordinary anger which I felt to be, in part at least, a projection of her own feelings, whilst Lesley herself was apparently totally unconcerned. It was as if I was to be discarded as she felt she had been. I was to be rendered useless by her attacks on my capacity to think about and under-stand her pain. In her turn Lesley would become like one of the adults whom she had felt did not care and had no concern.

However, held within the content of her activities was a much more vulnerable Lesley. Sitting on the window sill she would reassure herself and me, 'It's not far if I fall out.' Her talk was of accidents and she told me about a girl who had fallen off a roof, adding anxiously that she was not responsible. She often sang about a little girl who had died and wanted to go to heaven to be a queen, but God had said that as she had been naughty she would have to go to hell.

In these and other sequences with constant themes of death, punishment and falling, Lesley was incessantly telling me that she did not feel safely held or contained by me, so that she had to manage on her own. In this telling she also seemed to be re-experiencing some of the despair of the baby Lesley with a mother who had not held her safely in her care, and who by dying was felt to have dropped her altogether.

As the Easter gap approached, Lesley's feelings of precariousness were exacerbated by the pending holiday, and by her concern about whether I would return or would just disappear out of her life as had happened with the previous therapist. But it was possible to feel just before the holiday that she was allowing both of us to be slightly more in touch with her needy self, although mostly these needs were difficult to acknowledge. If anyone was to feel deprived, she implied, it would have to be me. There was also at this time a reorganisation in the home which Lesley described as the home 'breaking up', and her play now turned to a preoccupation with reorganising the furniture of the room in different combinations. Then suddenly towards the end of the session she spilled out the little family of dolls and wooden bricks from her drawer, and played out a scene which I felt to be a most poignant and moving statement about her life.

The fall Six bricks were arranged in pairs on top of each other
and she told me that this was a shop. Above this she placed a roof
brick and balanced precariously on the roof she set the girl doll
that she always used to represent herself. Lesley said, 'The little
girl is going to fall off.' She then arranged the other dolls around
in a circle. These were relatives, including an aunt and uncle.
No dolls were designated as either mother or father. They all stood
around watching. The scene was like a crowd gathering, each doll
fetching another saying, 'Look, come and see.' No one did anything,
just watched. At last the little girl fell and Lesley called out, 'She's
dead, there's blood!.' Immediately one couple began to argue, the
woman blaming the man but nothing was done. Then the aunt came
forward, picked up the little girl and hugged her, telling the others
that she was not dead after all. The aunt then called to a woman
who joined the two of them, while the rest of the figures went off
into the house. Lesley began humming,

> I love you, I miss you
> Ever since I met you
> You mean so much to me.

This sequence contained within it Lesley's essential experience of
parting and loss. It conveyed the experience of an infant part
which, when it did not feel held securely by those who were her
carers, was lost; and that this loss was felt by Lesley's infant self
as if it were her own death. But there was hopefulness in this
sequence too. There was someone to pick her up, her aunt; and
I thought there was also hope that I too might be able to hold her
and her secret despair. She had tested my capacities to the full in
the months before; she had made me experience what it felt like
to be dropped, kept out and treated as an object of scorn. I had
survived her attack and I think this had enabled her to let me
begin to share the pain with her, and so perhaps to begin to bear
an acknowledgment of it inside herself.
During the last few days before the holiday Lesley's sessions
carried the same moving message. Most of her play was with the
dolls which she arranged in different combinations of couples.
Before leaving she wrapped each doll individually in plasticine and
laid them side by side. Only the aunt and uncle doll were wrapped
as a couple. The baby doll was wrapped last, and after some
hesitation was placed next to the wrapped Lesley doll. A blanket
was then placed over them all. As she helped me put them away in
her drawer she told them that they could wake up in two weeks'
time. Then she handed the plasticine parcel over to me with a
reminder that I was to be careful not to break them.
I thought that this showed some acknowledgment that the baby
and child parts of Lesley did belong to each other, that there was
a place where they could be looked after and brought together,
and that she cared about this.
On her return Lesley took the plasticine off the figures telling
me that the baby was cold and that it needed its clothes. The dolls

were then used to depict a scene of a girl who had nearly died, having fallen off a cliff and caught pneumonia. The girl was put to bed. This time there were carers; at first a boy and girl knelt by the bed but then other members of the family arrived and I was told that they were all looking after the girl.

It seemed to me that Lesley had come back not only with some sense of continuity in spite of the break in treatment, but that she had also been able to tell me how the break itself had been experienced by the baby part of her. At this level she had felt exposed and left out in the cold, as if there had been a terribly dangerous fall which might have resulted in death. In contrast to the earlier story of the fall, this time the images of caring 'siblings' and parent figures were evidently felt to be very close and present in her mind.

Later on in the year, in the summer, Lesley began to surprise me by sometimes listening in a far more responsive way. Just before the summer break she took all the contents out of her drawer, cleaned it, which she had never done before, and then tried to curl up inside it herself. Still she found such moods difficult to sustain and when I commented on her wish to make sure that I would be all right, able to look after her and keep her place safe, she quickly became angry and dismissive.

The cross It was not until nearer the end of the year, in late autumn, that Lesley's deeper feelings and anxieties were expressed in a session in which she was able to sustain this mood with far less disruption than on previous occasions. She dared to show some of her feelings about her dead mother. In a most dramatic way she told of her sorrow and anger, of her phantasy about her mother in heaven, together with hints of wondering about her father – who he was, and whether he was alive or dead. It raised the possibility that forgiveness might lead to a mitigation of tormented feelings as a step towards integration and growth.

This session began with Lesley singing a carol, 'A Partridge in a Pear Tree'. She was drawing as she sang, but the song became muddled and the paper became messier, it was then torn and finally thrown away.

'I know what I'll do.' She folded a piece of paper and began to draw a star and a king. As she painted she sang 'Silent Night, Holy Night', in a way which balanced between seriousness and mockery. I picked up the tenderness and, no sooner had I done so, than she began to make jokes with the singing. I talked about the other side of her feelings, the tenderness and vulnerability. Lesley became very serious and looked at her painting, and then began to talk quickly and urgently. She wondered how it was, how you knew how many kings there were – were there three, two or one king? 'We don't know, do we? Maybe no one knows. The Bible says so, but that's a story, there is no one left alive to know. Who is there in the Bible: Jesus, Mary, the Kings, Joseph – maybe he is or not – Peter, Paul. . . . In school the teacher asked what was the most important three-letter word in the Bible. I thought it was

"thee" at first, but then I said I know, it's "God". I like Jesus,
he is kind, nice and good. He cured the little girl who was crying
because her sister died. He touched her. My mother and grandfather are dead. My father – I don't know, maybe he is, maybe he
isn't. Perhaps Jesus will ask my mother to his birthday? I'd like
to see Jesus and meet him. But he's dead and I'd have to be dead
too, wouldn't I? And I'm not, I'm alive,' and her voice was full of
sadness.

Lesley went back to her painting and on a clean sheet of paper
began to draw the outline of a cross, the figure and the crown
of thorns: 'I must remember to put the nails in and blood from the
nails. I would not like to be dead.' And then, with her voice
raised: 'One thing he said was silly: He said forgive them for they
know not what to do [sic]. I'd kill them – how could he say that,
stupid, I'd kill them all.' She began to colour in red all around the
figure, she blacked the outline in again and finally the body was
given two breasts.

Lesley left the picture on the table and climbed on to the window
sill and drew the curtain so that she was behind it. As she did so,
she said to me, 'You can still see me, can't you?'

In this brief account of Lesley's first year of psychotherapy with
me, I have tried to convey a picture of her internal world and the
way in which this was communicated to me. I have tried to describe
something of her rapid fluctuations of mood with the intensity of
warmth and the strength of her needs and longings, and of the
reverse, the vicious attacks on herself and on me at any acknow-
ledgments of these. Constantly the message was that it is not safe
to trust, that she could manage on her own, that was how she
survived.

In the description of the Christmas session perhaps we can dis-
cern a central thread in her development. She reveals how the
figure of Jesus represents her thoughts about her dead mother.
There is pity and pain for the suffering but anger too, as with
Jesus; yet at the same time remembering the kind Jesus who cured
the weeping child and who is also the one who forgives and is
resurrected. As she becomes more in touch with her anger towards
the good and loved figure and more open to the sadness, thoughts
of forgiving and being forgiven seem nearer and a softer, more
receptive Lesley comes to life. As I recognised with her such
moments of being serious, of tenderness, happiness, of caring,
and of pain and loss, and stayed with her as she pulled away into
her many protective devices, there seemed a hope that a more
integrated and genuinely trusting Lesley could now begin to thrive
and grow.

3   STICKING: MORE GIRLS IN CARE

The little girl described in the previous chapter had suffered
traumatic experiences in her early life. Yet she did have some early
experience together with her mother in contrast to some other
children in the series who had had little or no experience of individual mothering as babies, having spent their earliest months in
hospital or residential nursery, where frequent changes of staff
were likely to have made significant emotional attachments difficult.
Some of these, especially the girls, were quite clinging, craving for
affection in a pathetic or appealing way, but there was often a flat,
superficial quality to the contact they made with their therapists.
Foster and houseparents too sometimes had difficulty in establishing
deeper relationships with them.

Katy was just such a little girl. She was in foster-care when she
came into psychotherapy but there was a danger of foster breakdown.

Katy
Katy started life in an incubator, two months premature, weighing
only two pounds. Within four months she had been readmitted twice
to hospital, first with gastroenteritis, then with multiple bruising.
She was placed in a residential nursery and then a children's
home until foster-parents were found for her when she was 3. She
has been able to remain with this couple, who have three children
of their own, two born after Katy's arrival into the family.

She was just 5 when she started once-weekly therapy though
she looked two years younger, very thin, rigid, and with a
pathetic quality about her. I felt warmly towards this intelligent-
looking little blonde girl and yet I felt I could not really reach her.
She had been referred to the clinic two years after the foster-
placement because of her small size, poor eating habits, soiling
and whimpering. These problems were difficult for her foster-
mother to cope with, as were Katy's continual demands for attention.
The foster-mother, too, found Katy unreachable in some way and
was worried by her lack of affection. In fact she showed many of
the characteristics typical of children brought up in an institutional
setting without the opportunity for the development of deeper
attachments.

This was shown in the very ready way she followed me, a
stranger, at our first meeting, hardly looking back at her foster-
mother. She was unusually forthcoming and confiding in the first
few sessions. She made a lot of 'books' although she could not
write, scribbling as she said, 'This is my name and this is something

else about me.' As she cut and stuck paper, she talked about not
having a real mother or her own home. She drew a little girl, herself, and started colouring her, saying the figure was wet from the
glue and a 'mess'. She drew another picture of herself, making a
face in a little piece of paper, but again, as she was doing the
mouth, she made a mess. She finally managed to do a picture which
she liked, drawn on a paper with lines representing the therapist's
other children. This time she deliberately coloured a 'mess' inside
'her' body. After this she needed to clean up and to throw little
pieces of paper into the waste-paper basket. But there was one
long piece which she wanted to keep, colouring it red and black,
saying, when questioned, that it was 'a baby who is dead'.

I would like to stress that Katy seemed able, from the very
beginning, to establish a relationship with me as a therapist to
whom she could communicate her phantasies. Katy's drawing and
cutting could be understood as her way of conveying her image of
herself – a mess, fit only for the bin – the soiling, dirty child,
perhaps, who was afraid of what would happen to her at the clinic.
The piece of paper she needed to keep, possibly the dead baby
aspect of herself, shown to me in this early session, might convey
her hope that the therapy might bring this dead baby to life.

Falling – a recurrent theme – In her second session, Katy tried to
make a cylinder but could not manage it and complained of not
having a 'space' to put the small pieces of paper that stood for
herself. In the fifth session, Katy made a calendar and in each
square wrote her own name instead of the date. She then edged
each square with a lot of sellotape. The calendar seemed connected
with the therapy times and perhaps expressed not only a wish for a
session every day but the beginning of a feeling of being held in
the therapy, of finding a 'space' in the therapist's mind for herself.
In later sessions, Katy often asked me to hold, not her, but the
chair or table on which she sat. It seemed remarkable to me that
she appeared to feel safer, and more held by an inanimate object,
without direct human contact. Could this be related to the incubator
in which she spent so many weeks after birth?

At other times she would push against my knee and complain,
'Why are you touching me? Don't touch me,' thus showing a desire
for contact as well as a fear of it. Often she felt held only precariously, fearing she would fall down. On such occasions she
became stiff, holding herself, as it were, and rocking, like a baby
left to her own devices. I felt very helpless at these times and
painfully unable to meet her needs. Similar feelings were aroused
in the staff of the children's home and in the foster-mother, so
that they were often despairing and immobilised by guilt. Katy
tended to elicit painful feelings in others, while, especially in
the initial phase of treatment, being apparently devoid of them
herself. She was projecting quite powerfully her suffering and
distress.

A vivid example of how Katy needed to hold herself together
when feeling unheld by me came when I had to tell her about the

first holiday break in the treatment, which, unfortunately, coincided
with her foster-mother's being in hospital. When told about my
holiday, Katy stood stiffly, her body braced and arms held against
her sides - as if she would fall to pieces unless she held herself so.
She took out a piece of paper and drew a house with three chimneys,
four windows and a door, but without any floor. Did she feel the
ground was being taken from beneath her feet? She then drew a
picture of herself outside the house, in mid air, and then a black-
board (it was also her first school holiday). Sky was added, but
still no ground. She realised the omission when I talked to her
about it and became more relaxed. She put the picture in her box
and decided to make a book. Again she could not manage it, but
went on cutting and cutting. After we had discussed her feeling of
being dropped or falling down, Katy was able to draw a different
house and little girl, this time with a deep border around the picture, as if to make a strong 'incubator' able to hold her and me
during the holiday. But when it was time to go, at the end of the
session, the little girl was crossed out, again conveying the feeling
of not belonging anywhere.

For a while in this session, Katy seemed to feel 'held' by my
understanding, only to feel dropped again at the end when I was
no longer to be concretely present. She was not yet able to keep
inside herself a concept of someone who had space and thought
for her, an internal figure that could sustain and hold her. She
had missed, in her earliest weeks, the holding arms and attention
of the 'ordinary devoted mother', as described by Winnicott (1968)
which might have helped her to develop a feeling of containment
within herself. Instead she had experienced a mechanical, transparent, hard container - the incubator, which could not have had
the capacity for 'reverie' described by Bion (1962) as an important
ingredient in the mother's receptivity to her infant's emotional
states (see Chapters 1 and 9). Katy felt she had no space for the
pieces of paper representing herself, no container, no mother's
receptive understanding which could modify her anxieties, her
primitive terror of falling endlessly, as if there were no bottom or
ground. Katy could only evacuate such feelings and by such expulsion lost touch with them completely, leaving her personality
shallow and impoverished.

Her soiling might be understood as a concrete expression of this
endless evacuation and inability to contain her own unwanted pro-
ducts and feelings. She felt herself uncontained, leaking and
uncared for - in her words 'a mess'. She used to say, 'Who cares?
I don't care. You don't care, do you?' or, 'I never cry. I don't
cry. Its OK.' It was I then who was the one to experience the pain.

Katy's 'I don't care' seemed to be her attempt to protect herself
from the pain of caring, in much the same way as Lesley in the
previous chapter and Tom and Keith in the next tried to disguise
their vulnerability. But there was a more transparent, pathetic
quality about Katy, perhaps because her attempts to hold herself
together seemed so painfully inadequate - the defence seemed very
thin. It was rather like her attempts to stop herself falling by hold-

ing herself stiff and rigid. Bick (1968, pp. 484-6) has described
this kind of muscular holding, which the infant may develop as a
substitute for the feeling of being held by an attentive mother, as
a 'second skin' - a pseudo kind of containment. Katy indeed quite
concretely had skin troubles and expressed her feelings through
her skin. Whenever she felt dropped, she came to the session with
dry skin round her eyes and mouth. Her skin was breaking out,
or she came with a wound. Even her skin seemed thin and inadequate (in contrast to the apparently thick skin of Henry's 'doubly
deprived' patient in Chapter 1).

Katy could not hold on to her own work, throwing away her
drawings during sessions (as she herself felt thrown away as an
infant?). When I discussed this with her I felt she needed me to
provide a container, which I did concretely in the form of a plastic
bag for her to put her work in. Katy seemed relieved, perhaps that
I at least did want to hang on to what she had produced. In the
last session before the holiday she even put her box of toys inside
the bag 'to make it stronger'.

Further development As the therapy progressed, Katy gradually
began to develop more trust in my ability to receive and understand
some of her confused feelings. For a time I had to be the messy
baby, while she was the busy, angry mother. However she was
sometimes able to ask for help in clearing up and to allow herself
to be the child. She was very confused about the eye operation
she had during the course of the therapy. It was experienced as
punishment, as being sent away. I too had to have my eyes covered,
and to experience the pain and fear. Working on these feelings, in
preparation for the separation from the therapy and the ordeal in
hospital, led to a growing trust that I would keep her in mind and
be there when she returned, while also feeling that she would be able
to remember me. She was beginning to have the feeling of an internal
holding mother figure, even though this figure was still quite fragile.

Her growing confidence and trust in the therapist exposed Katy
to pangs of jealousy and envy of my other relationships and despair at being left out. She projected powerfully feelings of inadequacy into me, at times when she attacked and destroyed everything,
breaking things, dirtying the room, herself and me. She had a
phantasy of having a baby inside her who was eating her up. She
had to starve this baby and this seemed to be connected with her
poor eating and thinness, as well as her jealousy of her foster
mother's own children. It took a long time to work on Katy's confused feelings. Sometimes the sessions were very painful, Katy
wanting to trust me but not being able to. But even in the very
disruptive and angry sessions, Katy conveyed somehow her request
for help. It seemed important for her to have a therapist able to
maintain boundaries, to cope with her confusion and destruction,
and this firmness and limit setting gradually took on the meaning of
a father who can help the mother to look after the child.

Katy made gradual progress in therapy. As she came to realise there was a space in my mind where I could think about her and hold her in my attention, she was able to do the same. She was able to be a bit more contained, and with this, about a year after starting therapy, came an improvement in the soiling and eating. The foster-mother also reported she was able to cry. The 'don't care' attitude seemed to be changing. There was a great deal more work to be done and therapy continued for a further two years, when it had to end because of external circumstances. I felt this was premature in view of Katy's very early deprivation and the fragility of her inner world. I can only hope that she was able to build something in the therapeutic work which can be preserved and which will be a source of inner sustenance in the future.

GIRLS AND BOYS

Children like Katy have problems with identification, with taking inside good internal figures. They find it hard to make deep relationships, but instead tend to relate to the surface qualities of people, a kind of 'adhesive identification' (a concept developed by Bick and described by Meltzer (1975). They stick themselves or cling by means of mimicry.

Many of the girls in this series tended to be conforming in this way and to get by unnoticed in school and elsewhere. In contrast, the boys in general showed more aggressive and anti-social behaviour. There have been exceptions however. The violent attacks of 9-year-old Cindy on the therapist and on the room made her very hard to contain in treatment (Tustin, 1960) and in contrast Mathew (see Chapter 11) was a very unaggressive little boy.

One might make a broad distinction between the boys' generally more open and active attacks on or defences against developing close relationships, and the girls' more inward or 'passive resistance' style of response. This would conform with some commonly accepted expectations of differences of temperament between boys and girls, but how far this may be a reflection of social pressures and how far of individual disposition is of course part of a much wider issue.

Wolkind and Rutter (1973), in a survey of 10-11-year-old children who had been in care, found a strong association between long-term family disruption and anti-social disorder in boys but not in girls. It was not clear from this study whether girls could be supposed to be less affected by family disruption than boys, or whether, as Wolkind (1977b) suggests, they do have high rates of psycho-social problems later in life. Further work by Wolkind, Hall and Pawlby (1977) indicates that girls from disrupted family backgrounds may, when they become mothers, interact significantly less with their babies than mothers who have not had such early separations.

It could be that girls react rather differently from boys to the lack of a mother's holding arms and caring preoccupation when they are very tiny. The therapists' observations of the kinds of

relationships which some of the girls make over a period of time, in
psychotherapy, suggest that not having been 'held' at a crucial
stage of development may lead to an impairment of the capacity to
take in, grasp and hold on to thoughts, feelings, memories and
experience – the 'in one ear and out of the other' kind of phenomenon. There is no feeling of depth or of an inner world or space.
Everything falls out or is dropped, sometimes concretely expressed
by soiling. We can see how they might grow up to have difficulties
with mothering their own children. It must be hard to be a mother
who can hold and care for a child when you do not have a feeling
of a good internal mother inside to sustain you. It is hardly surprising if these girls grow up to become mothers who let their own
children slip into care, so perpetuating the cycle of deprivation.
In this connection it is interesting to note that Cindy, who gave her
therapist such a bad time and whose very caring social worker has
kept in touch with her over many years, is now a successful mother
of two children.

The appealing behaviour of some of the girls tended to elicit more
attempts at help and caring from the environment (in contrast to
the 'doubly deprived', hard-to-reach boys), but they were often
experienced as unrewarding, unable to hold on to and to develop
what they received. Such girls could end up being rejected like the
boys. This process is vividly described by Eileen's therapist.

Eileen
Eileen could hardly have had a more deprived start to her life.
She was in the care of the local authority from birth: she never
had any contact with her mother, though her father kept up a little
irregular communication. She was born two months prematurely,
and spent a long time in an incubator. Her survival was a matter of
touch and go, and she remained a weakly child, ill on and off and
in hospital several times in her first two years. So for the first two
years of her life Eileen had no single person who was responsible
for her care.

After this Eileen was able to stay in the same residential nursery
till she was 6, and the Matron there took a great interest in her
and kept it up long after Eileen left the nursery. At age 6 Eileen
went to a children's home, and she was fortunate to be placed in
one where the same housemother stayed in charge for many years.
So Eileen at last had pretty continuous care, and people tried to
take seriously the job of bringing her up. Her social worker, too,
was of years' standing, and her school helpfully tried to offer
special attention of various kinds. But the all-too-noticeable fact
was that Eileen could make hardly any use of what was offered to
her.

When Eileen began therapy at the age of 14, she was regarded
as being nearly impossible to live with. There was a feeling that
she would have been ejected from the home if there had been anywhere else obvious to send her. The complaints from the staff were
overwhelming. It was not that there were accounts of violent or

even grossly naughty behaviour, but the general idea (put across
with intensity) was that Eileen was unbearable because she made
everyone feel such a hopeless failure. Nobody felt they could get
through to her; nothing satisfied her; no occupation held her; no
treat pleased her. Every effort to help her fell through, like water
poured into a sieve. There was one specific complaint. Eileen was
said to use the bathroom towels for wiping her bottom on. This
upset and preoccupied the housemother very much. Thus the
picture of Eileen at this time was of a blank, flat, empty girl without much in the way of feelings of her own, while all about her the
people who were trying to look after her were full to the top with
worry, frustration and anger.

When I first met Eileen I was taken aback to see how small she
was. I had no difficulty in imagining her as a premature baby. She
looked no more than 8 or 9 years old. She was scrawny, meagre
and under-sized. Her whole way of behaving matched the physical
impression she gave of being a much younger child than she really
was. Though there was no hint that Eileen literally did not eat,
it certainly seemed that what she took in could not be nourishing
her. Similarly, of course, she could not make use of education to
enlarge her mind or of experience to make her grow in character.
Things went in at one end and out at the other without doing her
much good. Even the business of dirtying the towels fits in here.
While no one felt that he or she could give Eileen a nice meal she
would enjoy, or a useful lesson she would digest and remember,
everyone involved with her was aware of a broadcasting of misery,
a sort of rubbishy residue of anger and fright and anxiety which
seemed to emanate from Eileen and which was also given perceptible
form by the soiling of the towels - something which upset every-
body else while leaving Eileen unmoved.

It was as if Eileen had succeeded in putting her nasty feelings
into other people. They were having her feelings for her. But
this process left her not only empty of bad feelings, but empty of
good things as well. Consequently she was flat, shallow and
superficial. When she began seeing me regularly for therapy, Eileen
chattered away brightly enough, or so it seemed on the surface.
She prattled on like a small child, not at all like a 14-year-old girl
meeting that rather unknown quantity, a psychotherapist. I felt
I was being regarded as a very temporary phenomenon - someone
who probably would never be seen again. Eileen showed no nervous-
ness, no real unease and no curiosity about who I was or what I
might be for. Early on in the therapy she drew a house with lots of
carefully coloured furniture but no people; it had no front, like
those dolls' houses which have no facade. While she drew she
talked ceaselessly, and she did not look at me, but out of the big
plate-glass window at the gardens. It occurred to me that Eileen
was clearly trying to 'get on well' with me. Getting on well with me
did not, apparently, mean talking actually with me, asking me
things, expecting that I might comment or answer and that she
might be affected one way or another by what I said. It seemed
more a matter of filling her ears with her own chatter while looking

at the pretty garden and the pretty house she drew.

I began to realise that her chatter was only making sense in a superficial way. The anecdotes she told were a hopelessly confused mixture of fact and fiction; what had happened to her on the bus was all muddled up with what might have happened to her on the bus. I had no way of telling what was real and what was not, and neither had Eileen, it seemed. Nor was she telling stories which had a proper plot. Incidents were stuck together; there was no logic and no plan. It did seem, however, that this talk had a function. Essentially, it was to keep me quiet, to stop me having any disturbing ideas or making any disturbing comments. If what I said impinged on Eileen, if it could not be smoothed over and quickly amalgamated into her narrative, then it was felt to be upsetting and even dangerous. That is to say, any indication I gave that I was alive and thinking, independent and unpredictable, represented a threat. It seemed that Eileen could feel moderately comfortable as long as she glued her eyes to the window and kept me at arm's length. This made me think of her earliest months in the incubator when nobody held her or came close to her, and when she saw everything through glass. She continued to do this, any- way, because she wore spectacles; and she had a characteristic way of looking at me, as though her gaze stayed on the surface of my eyes and did not penetrate. Another preference she had was for television over real life. The people on the television, safe at a distance and behind glass, seemed to make her feel more lively and cheerful than any flesh-and-blood person did.

We might ask, why did Eileen not get over the experience of her earliest months? Why did she, apparently, stick to a way of relating to people superficially and at a distance? The answer may lie in what happened to her once she was out of the incubator; or rather, what failed to happen to her. Eileen did not have a mother whose attention was for Eileen alone. She got a series of changing nurses. The constant factor in each feed was not the person - a mother whose voice, glances, ways of doing things all sprang from some- thing in her which stayed individual and unchanging. The constant factor was the bottle (another hard, inanimate, even glassy object) and the face, voice, manner, way of holding Eileen changed every time. There was no single person to receive her communications of fright or misery and to puzzle away at them, worrying and trying to understand. Nor did Eileen's first smiles perform the function of binding a mother affectionately close to her. From the baby Eileen's point of view (no matter how wordless, unformulated and infantile that was) it must have seemed that if she cried or broad- cast distress, people went away; and if she felt nice or cooed and smiled, people went away just as inevitably. No one kept coming back as in ordinary circumstances a mother does even when she is worried or cross, and nobody was cheered up in a more than superficial way by Eileen when she was happy.

As the therapy went on, Eileen began to derive some benefit from the regularity of session times and from the way in which the room and the setting in general was as reliable and constant as could be

managed. She felt held by the structure afforded by the treatment
and perhaps by my attempts to struggle away at understanding her
communications. Gradually traces of emotion and thought appeared
in her; at the same time, the anxiety and complaints in the home
died down to a more manageable level. The soiling of the towels had
stopped and Eileen was a little less dependent on simply getting rid
of her feelings. However, I had plenty of chance to experience what
it had been that the staff of the home had been worrying about.
Eileen's development can be seen if one contrasts how she felt
about two Christmas holidays – the first and third of treatment.
The first Christmas was hardly noticed. The way Eileen talked about
it, you would have thought she and I had had exactly the same
Christmas. She asked me if I had a turkey, said she had; asked me
if I had a tree, said she had. There was no feeling that she and I
had been parted from each other, no idea of missing me or of missing out on anything. Two years later she crept back with a terrible
cold, full of moans and miseries; the lucky ones had been invited
out, but not her; she had quarrelled with people the whole time and
the housemother had accused her of dirtying the towels again. I
tried to talk and think with her about how miserable and left out
she had felt. But the feeling which lodged in me – and this is the
sort of feeling the staff used to get – was of utter disheartenment
and gloom. I felt a hopeless failure, especially when I heard about
those towels. It took me a little time to realise that these were feelings of Eileen's which had communicated themselves to me, rather
than rational judgments on how the therapy was going.

However, although progress was slow, Eileen seemed to become
distinctly more capable of experiencing her own emotions. She
filled out physically and mentally. She grew quite tall and well-
rounded in body, and she added gradually to her repertoire of
thoughts and ideas. The housemother was surprised to find that
Eileen was avidly reading paperback romances, and to find that
Eileen had lots of memories of early days in the children's home
to contribute to conversation. Eileen's social worker was touched as
well as surprised to be bought a bar of chocolate. People stopped
thinking that to discuss Eileen's future with her was pointless, as
many small incidents such as those above gave convincing evidence
that Eileen was becoming more of a three-dimensional person.

But when the time came for her to leave school, Eileen was badly
upset. She proceeded to a college of further education. The implication that she was growing up alarmed her and the casual college
atmosphere was experienced by her as frighteningly sexual. She
was in and out of trouble, including some stealing, and she could
not bring herself to attend the college regularly. In relation to
this one might conjecture that Eileen would have done much better
if she had had some help earlier in her life. If she had made the
same progress between the ages of 4 and 7 as she did between the
ages of 14 and 17 she might have been able to look forward to many
more years of relatively protected development in which to consoli-
date the gains made. As it was, Eileen was put out into the adult
world all unequipped.

Nevertheless, she was not quite as unequipped as people had feared she was going to be. Eileen survived the college year without anything irrevocably harmful taking place. Throughout this time she was able to make attempts to recount, discuss, think about and own what was happening to her. At the end of the year, not many months before her therapy ended, she was able - to everyone's surprise - to go to a job centre, apply for and get a job. This job she only held for six weeks: she was kindly dismissed as not being quite up to it. But she managed to get another, and the general feeling was that even though serious setbacks might yet come about, Eileen had got further than anybody had expected she would get.

A mixture of aggressive and clinging, appealing behaviour was shown by 11-year-old Chris. The following picture outlined by her therapist illustrates a number of the problems which commonly arouse concern in children's homes.

Chris
Chris was referred for psychotherapy because she displayed promis-cuous, exhibitionist behaviour, exposing and manipulating her breasts. When she also began stealing money, both in the school and at the home, the staff were additionally alarmed to discover that this money was being spent on a secret hoard of baby food and baby clothes. They considered that there was a serious risk of her seeking sexual encounters.

Chris's background was different from many of the other children in the series in that she was not received into care until the age of 8, when she was found to be unmanageable at home. It seemed that she was emotionally rejected by her mother who had been longing for a boy. Although very little is known about the quality of her early care, there was some evidence that she had become the recipient of negative feelings within the family, who maintained very little contact with her after she came into care. She had remained in the same children's home for three years, but there had been many changes of staff.

In manner and appearance Chris had considerable charm, and despite her frequently defiant or arrogant behaviour aroused maternal feelings and concern in all those who were professionally involved in her care. There were therefore some healthy and hope-ful qualities in her personality which enabled her to enlist and to make some use of help. However her ways of seeking for help could be misdirected in many ways.

Chris was attached to two housemothers but later began to split off all her bad feelings into the one most involved in her care, while keeping only good feelings for the other. This created diffi-culties between them, which Chris tried to exploit in a manipulative way and similarly attempted to stir up divisions between the clinic and the home. At such times the importance of the clinic social worker's contribution in having established a helpful relationship with the children's home was most clearly evident. He had kept in touch in a supportive way from the date of the referral, although

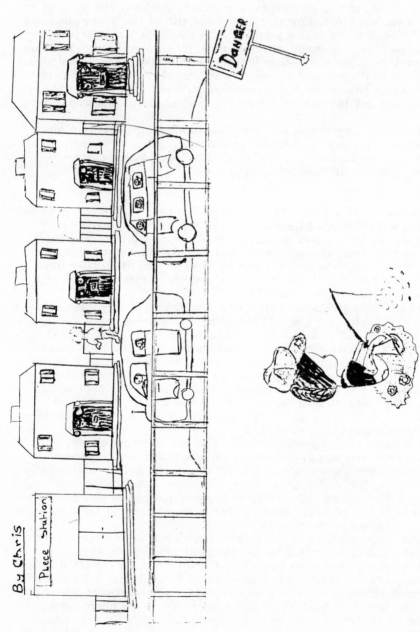

Figure 3.1

there had been a long interval before the beginning of therapy.

Another characteristic feature was the pressure of Chris's wish to obtain some concrete evidence of care, and most insistently the wish for a place not just in her therapist's thoughts and time and concern, but in her home - to be adopted or fostered. During some two and a half years in psychotherapy there unfolded a picture of the kind of inner images which were leading Chris in a childish search for some idealised phantasy family, or troubling her with fears of hostile and persecuting figures.

At the very beginning of therapy she drew a picture of a solitary girl in the middle of a lake (see Figure 3.1). There is a sign marked 'Danger' nearby. The figure is childish, but somehow sophisticated, a girl wearing a 'rakish' peaked cap. There is an air of bravado, and of an ambiguous sexuality. It is not clear who or what is in danger. This part of the picture is surrounded by a fence, and on the other side there is a street with families in motor cars and in the distance a row of houses which seem to stare outwards with sinister forbidding human features. In the corner a police station is marked 'Plece'.

Is she telling us how lonely and frightened she feels as she attempts to set up her proud phantasy of self-sufficiency, of the way in which this phantasy cuts her off from the happily enclosed families? Perhaps these houses with their darkly closed faces are images of a series of 'house' mothers and fathers whom she has passed on her way without finding someone to take in and contain her emotional needs, challenges, and anxieties. Somewhere in the corner, though, is her plea for help and protection, the hope or expectation that somewhere there is the strength to hold and control internal and external destructive forces.

One of the ways in which Chris used her therapy to convey her feelings was through games in which she reversed the roles of adult and child, treating her therapist in a painfully rejecting way, making her feel like a neglected infant whose mother had just no time for her at all. Talking about 'baby feelings' was not enough, Chris needed to demonstrate them actively, and to enact the mother-infant relationship - with all the practical attentions and confused emotionality that this meant for her - sometimes playing the 'mummy' role and sometimes being the baby Chris. She would bring me bottles and plastic pants, but then in another session when she was baby she brought into the open the whole area of her deep-seated confusion between the mother-infant couple and the mother-father couple. She showed me her bottom, as if asking me to change her nappy, then said that I wanted to 'have sex with her' because I 'was treating her like a baby'.

This eroticised quality of Chris's way of relating to her therapist could be considered partly as an aspect of her urge to manipulate, seduce and control the adult figures in her life. As a denial of her state of dependence on the adult's care, the confusion served to make her feel as if this was a relationship between peers with equal needs. Though some such phantasies seem to form a part of every infant's complex experiences of being loved, fed and physically cared for, their adolescent emergence in Chris was unusually marked and concretely physical.

When her sessions with me became important to her, she needed to touch me, wanting me to hold her as if to prove that I would not send her away, reject her as her parents had done. She seemed unable to experience contact and acceptance in terms of understanding and empathy, perhaps because it threatened her with the awareness of emotional pain. At times when such an awareness seemed near she would quickly turn to her own body for comfort and masturbate during her sessions. Once Chris told me that she had to masturbate because she was 'all dry inside'. This 11-year-old girl seemed to be expressing something sad and lonely, an unsatisfied thirst, a longing to feel alive inside herself, to feel loved and cherished as an infant.

Figure 3.2

By turning to masturbation she was attempting to exclude deeper
feelings and to focus instead on physical sensation alone, denying
the need for or the meanings implicit in personal relationships. As
these feelings were dealt with in therapy the promiscuous sexual
behaviour in her life outside began to recede.

Chris's modes of thinking and behaving illustrate vividly multiple
confusions over relationships between persons and, parallel with
this, confusions about her own body, as if somehow parts of herself
could sometimes seem to be a feeding breast or a penis or else
represent a baby or a masculine self. In this way she sometimes
contrived to maintain a phantasy of being like a self-sufficient
family all in one with instant answers to all her own needs.

One wondered whether in her infancy Chris felt cared for only in
terms of surface attentions to her physical requirements and never
experienced any intuitive sense of being held in her mother's
thoughts. This would have made it hard for her to feel that there
could be any sense of contact with her mother when she was
physically absent. Such doubts were given some support by an
extraordinary drawing which she produced when she had been in
therapy for about a year (Figure 3.2). The mother in this drawing
is a very flat, two-dimensional figure with no apparent capacity for
taking anything in. As Esther Bick (1968) has commented 'the
internal function of containing the parts of the self is dependent
initially on the introjection of an external object experienced as
capable of fulfilling this function.' The baby seems to be stuck on
to the surface of the mother and not in any sense held by her.

Where the baby's heart might be there is a house, as if this
expresses Chris's dawning awareness of some metaphor of the heart
as an inner capacity for containing and sheltering. Perhaps this
is linked with her experience of therapy, and although it seems
that the house is still empty, it is a beginning.

The mother's eyes are empty and her face expressionless, and
directed away from the baby. This flat, indifferent caricature
suggests that Chris may never have been able to take in the figure
of a mother who could take care of her and watch over her throughout her life. The baby too does not look towards the mother but
displays a penis while smiling in an odd, triumphant way. There is
no feeding relationship between them, and indeed the breasts and
nipples might equally appear to represent the penis. This drawing
would seem to confirm the earlier exchanges during Chris's
sessions which were reported above, in which it appeared that she
experienced a nurturing relationship in terms of a sexually exciting
one. A confusion of this kind would interfere with the development
of a true experience of an infant's dependent relationship with her
mother, and distort the processes of emotional growth.

One might wonder to what extent this drawing echoes some
memories of infancy, or whether it reflects certain aspects of
institutional care. It also raises the important question as to what
kind of mother she will be to her own baby.

Chris's case illustrates very clearly the problem of promiscuous
sexual behaviour which forms a serious risk for some adolescent
girls in care. Their precocious sexual behaviour is not the expression

of a mature or deep relationship with a partner, but a longing for physical contact in a predominantly infantile way. If they then become pregnant it often seems as if they are expecting that the baby will provide them with the 'mother-love' which they feel they have missed in their own lives. Often these young girls have so little capacity for mothering that unconsciously they soon feel themselves in rivalry with the baby. Major difficulties of this kind may result in neglect or inadequate caring and sometimes injury, eventually resulting in their infants being taken into care, as with Katy, and thus continuing a tragic cycle.

In Chris's case, however, there had begun to be signs of significant improvement, as the stealing ceased completely and she was no longer preoccupied with 'baby things'. However, as her attachment to her therapist grew she also began to experience the holiday breaks as increasingly painful, and shortly before a long summer break, she decided to break off treatment. Although she had been attending for two and a half years and had made considerable progress, one felt that some of her difficulties remained to be resolved. However, one may hope that in so far as she was able to enter into a communicative and understanding relationship with her therapist, that this might provide some protection against acting out all her anxieties, some basis for a move towards more genuine relationships in the future.

4 ABANDONED

The two boys described in this chapter exemplify the more
aggressive behaviour in therapy which characterised many of the
boys and a few of the girls. It might be speculated that, in some
cases, the fighting spirit indicated less emotional deadness than
seemed to be present in the more superficial personalities.

Like Chris, in the previous chapter, Tom appeared to experience
the nurturing relationship as a sexually exciting one, and indeed
unusual extremes of confusion as well as violence emerged in the
course of treatment.

Tom
Tom was the second child of a single parent, a mother who had
suffered severe deprivation in her own childhood. Little seems to
be known about his father who had never kept in touch, and the
other children in the family had different fathers. During his first
years of life there were frequent admissions to hospital, twice at
the mother's request, when she became afraid of harming him, and
he entered into care when he was 5 years old, while the other
children remained with their mother.

Because of continual soiling and wetting he was referred to the
clinic and began individual psychotherapy on the basis of three
sessions weekly when he was 8½ years of age. When I first met him
Tom was a strong, attractive boy, and I was struck by his beautiful dark and expressive eyes. Even at times of greatest aggressiveness during sessions later on, the glimpse of some helpless appeal
might suddenly light up in his eyes, though it would quickly dis-
solve again. This eye contact was especially important with Tom
since he often directed such a barrage of violent and obscene words
or physical aggression at me that any possibility of verbal communication would become completely shattered.

Confusion One thing which was striking from the beginning was
Tom's defensive confusion combined with an overt idealisation of
faeces. In his second session he made a drawing of a road and
described how it led to the 'bottom' where there was a 'cafe'. While
drawing he got up and went to the sink to drink, commenting on
the water which he said was 'dirty, like chocolate'. When I suggested that he seemed to be confusing something nourishing and good
like chocolate or maybe milk with some dirty stuff, Tom said very
assertively, 'Milk comes from the bosom-bottom, lemonade from the
willy, poos from the bum.'

The first weeks of therapy were also characterised by an urgent curiosity about me as a therapist and maternal figure, whom he suspected of being very preoccupied with someone or something else. But this curiosity conflicted with a fierce intolerance that drove him to reject forcibly anything I said which might put him in touch with his jealousy and with his unresolved infant needs.

The first break and the empty drawer Our first break in treatment was for the Easter holiday which unfortunately came early. When I referred to some evidence of his having phantasies that during his absence over this holiday other children might wish to share the little toys which I had provided for him, Tom took this in a very literal and concrete way. Lifting up the whole drawer in a jealous rage he flung almost the entire contents out of the window. Then with his characteristic need to blame, Tom turned on me complaining bitterly and hurling accusations. At the same time it became clear that he himself felt identified with the little ball which had also been thrown out; as he left at the end of his session, Tom looked outside on to the roof-ledge, exclaiming sadly 'poor ball'.

This first holiday break showed the extreme intensity of Tom's feelings and in this respect his reactions did not fit into the more common picture of the so-called 'institutionalised child', but revealed rather the presence of a deep and strong emotional life. Throughout the year which followed this incident, the toys, which I had in fact managed to rescue from the ledge, were not given back to Tom.

Although a casual return of the toys after a brief discussion and a brief interval could have made the situation considerably more comfortable for both Tom and his therapist, it would have meant colluding in a denial of the central importance of the emotional factors which the incident represented. It seemed crucial to maintain a very firm analytic technique if there was to be any hope of eventually helping this child to get in touch with, understand and be able to bear the powerful feelings which underlay his disturbed and violent behaviour. If I had accepted the discarding of the toys simply at face value it would in fact have deprived him of an opportunity to confront an important constellation of experiences within the comparatively protected therapeutic setting. By implication such a response would have appeared to confirm the toys as representing something in the nature of a substitute for, rather than a symbol only of the vital personal relationships which were being expressed through them at the time.

During this year Tom filled his sessions with endless grudges, not only the superficial ones, the demanding 'why don't you give me my toys back?', but now also the deeper, unresolved early ones. His feeling of being 'the bottom baby', as he often said when complaining that his drawer was the bottom one in the chest of drawers, emerged forcefully into the transference relationship with me as I was treated as being the second-class mother of the 'second-class baby', and he called me 'Mrs Pakiani', a distortion meant to imply a contemptuous combination of Pakistani and my own name.

As his denigration and destructive activities increased, I was often filled with despair, at times completely overwhelmed and shattered by the obscene and abusive language and aggressive behaviour. One could then indeed feel like a weak, denigrated mother with no strength or mental capacity to look after a baby who projected such feelings of violence and confusion that they sometimes seemed beyond the bounds of tolerance. It seemed then as if when he had thrown his little toys out of the window he had thrown away the affectionate, tender bits of his own self which we could not rescue and could not manage to integrate in any way.

During this period Tom spent most of his sessions walking along the window sill on to the tables and on top of the chest of drawers. When he began tearing pieces out of the ceiling with a pair of scissors it became physically impossible either to prevent or to stop this, or even to bring his session to an end at the point when his aggression became unmanageable. It seemed evident that Tom felt totally without any internal sense of a strong, responsible, paternal figure who could control his primitive infant self and help to make good the damage. He could neither find such an image within himself nor acknowledge or accept such a presence within his therapist. One day, though, as he stood on the window sill tearing at the ceiling, he challenged. 'You should stop me!' Then close to the summer break, looking at the devastated ceiling, he said quietly, 'We must have a man to fix it.'

However, the sadistic behaviour and phantasies were to return once again, and following a missed session he came back with a horrifying account of trying to murder a cat trapped in a hole, and in the same session suddenly produced a heavy metal marble from his pocket and threw it against the window, breaking the thick glass panel. At other times he made direct attacks on me, throwing a chair or urinating, trying to write on my clothes or to cut them. Sometimes his activities would take a slightly more symbolic form as when he put a lump of plasticine on the top of the door, frantically opening and shutting it, shredding the plasticine to pieces. I perceived this as being similar to the attack on the cat trapped in the hole, representing an attack on a phantasied baby inside my body, or on the other patients whom he imagined coming in and out of my room. Though he might gather the bits together again and make them whole, he would soon seem impelled to begin cutting them up once again. During this time it seemed as if Tom had been trapped in a very destructive state of mind, completely caught up in a vicious circle of escalating violence which could so easily be set in motion. Perhaps the sequence with the plasticine did indeed represent the destructiveness of his jealous rage followed by a wish to restore. This could very rapidly succumb to destructiveness again as images of strong, intact rivals might fill him with renewed rage and with fears of retaliation.

If there was any positive or loving message for me this was conveyed only through singing popular love-songs. In these he displayed the great confusion between the levels of his helpless infantile longing for nurture and care from mother, and his phantasies of seizing her love for himself as if he were a powerful sexual partner. Characters like Elvis Presley, Tom's greatest idol,

and Rudolph Valentino were introduced and good performances
produced. These loving sequences would alternate or be mixed with
obscene detailed descriptions of sexual intercourse and a particular
regressive kind of play during which he would build himself a kind
of shelter or enclosure and curl up, staying still for a little while.

The presenting problem of wetting and soiling was also brought
into the sessions. Sometimes he could not hold his urine, spilling a
few drops in the beaker or bin. This seemed to parallel his use of
the relationship with me in order to evacuate unbearable feelings,
rejection, humiliation, helplessness, hopelessness. In this way his
image of me was becoming so filled with pain and denigration that
the possibility of perceiving me as someone who might be able to
survive such an onslaught and might, indeed, nurture and help him
to grow, seemed very remote.

Beginning to change As we approached the summer break Tom's
anxieties began to take a new direction, appearing now in the form
of hypochondriacal fears. He complained, for instance, about his
eyes being sore, saying that he could not see properly. These
complaints had a new quality, an acknowledgment of vulnerability
and pain and a wish that he might be helped to get well. It had
become possible at this time for him to begin to listen to some discussion, not only about his eyes but also about thoughts and
feelings, imagination and understanding, and references to distinctions between physical care and the qualities of thoughtfulness and
concern.

There seemed to be some signs of a readiness to move on to
being in touch with speech as a more symbolic medium of communication and less as an evacuation of unthinking rage. In acknowledging his difficulties over distinguishing between these two ways of
functioning, it was possible to link this with his need for concrete
ways of expressing his feelings, as, for instance, in throwing out
his toys when hurt and angry, and similarly in his continual
demands for concrete indications of my concern for him. It seemed
possible also to start to differentiate more between the part of
him which was so easily overwhelmed by intense, primitive feelings
mixed up and confused with physical urges, and the more responsible, grown-up schoolboy Tom, who wished to grow and to develop.

At the time when his confusion was expressed and acted out in
his sexual phantasies I would attempt to describe how it seemed
that the little baby self in him was reacting towards me as a mother
figure in the therapeutic relationship. It was as if the presence of
a mother's breast might excite not only hunger and sensuality but
also envy and resentment towards the possessor of so much that he
perceived to be good and which he greatly desired. This had led
him into distorting the nurturing relationship into something dirty
and sexually twisted. There was also a demanding possessiveness
as if wanting to get right inside the mother figure instead of being
able to come to her, and to be fed and cared for as a separate
individual, infant or child.

At a deep level it still seemed that much of the time he was over-

whelmed by a terrible muddle between images of a mother's breast
and of his own bottom, and between the different parts of his own
body and their functions, so that his obscene use of language was
partially an expression of such confusion.

Although later he seemed to have begun to master some of these
difficulties and to be in greater control of the urge to express them
physically, the imminence of the next break, over Christmas, precipitated a degree of rage and excitement which culminated in his
actually seizing and turning on the fire-extinguisher in the corridor. A few days later he constructed what he described as a
'coffin for the baby' while curling himself up in his own drawer,
covered and tucked up as if to hibernate inside over the holiday.

Such fluctuations in Tom's mental and emotional state continued
to be a feature of my experience with him, though gradually the
violence and frequency of the acting out diminished and the ability
to think and to communicate in symbolic ways was increasingly
evident in his responses. As the little toys and their meaning for
him became once again a focus of our work and Tom seemed to wish
to have them back now, not only as concrete signs from me but
more as a means of expression and communication between us, I
replaced them in his drawer. Their reappearance was celebrated by
a very elated session with drawings of flags, a description of
Everest as the highest mountain, and passionate kisses for each of
the little toys.

For Tom, the meaning of his regained toys and their confirmation
of his growing capacity to express himself in more symbolic ways
went together with an increased capacity to hold on to more inside
himself, both physically and in his thinking. The wish to grow and
to develop began to emerge. At the beginning of the second year he
arrived carrying his new training shoes, and we talked about his
wish to 'train', to learn to talk to me, as it were, and before starting to play with his little toys, he asked me to sit nearer to him so
that I could watch him more closely.

By the end of the second year his continuous soiling and wetting
during the day disappeared although he would occasionally wet his
bed at night. Many changes, external and internal, seem to have
occurred during this time.

Very gradually he began to spend more and more time at home
with his mother and siblings, at times travelling on his own and
coming to his sessions without an escort from the children's home.
More recently he has left the children's home and has joined his
family to live with them. He is still attending a school for maladjusted children but now comes to his sessions on his own soon after
school, where his teacher reports that he is doing well. Although
at times he still has patches of negativism or withdrawal in his
sessions, and sometimes turns to violent outbursts, it is not so
difficult for me to contain him as in the past and certainly he has
become more able to contain himself.

Recently our sessions coincided for some time with those of a very
violent boy in the room next door. This boy often shouted and
knocked against our wall and the interference would be experienced

by Tom as such a provocation that at times it seemed almost
impossible to check Tom's wish to engage in a fight with him. Then
one day, during one of the most escalating outbursts from next
door, Tom, who had been shouting back from the opened window,
stopped and pointing in the direction of the noise, whispered to
me in a very concerned voice, 'He must be a very disturbed boy. . . .'

Another very disturbed and deserted boy was Keith who is described next. His therapist explores his development and his preoccupation with cruelty.

Keith

Keith was abandoned at birth by a mother who herself had been
abandoned. Little is known about his infancy, the first sixteen
months of which were spent in a residential nursery, except that he
was said to have screamed incessantly. He was fostered for a year
with a couple who had three children of their own, but as it became
increasingly evident that Keith was half coloured, the father of
the family rejected him. Keith lived in a children's home until a
second attempt was made to foster him when he was 4 years old,
but this broke down only five months later due, it was said, to the
bitter jealousy of other children in the foster-home. So Keith
returned to the children's home and began school just one month
later.

Not surprisingly, the headmistress of his infant school found
him 'anti-social and generally destructive, unable to make contact
with children or adults, frustrated by the slightest setback, and
usually alone'. Keith was referred to the clinic at this time, but
psychotherapy was not recommended. Rather it was felt that
support should be given to the people who were trying to care for
him at home and school. They were patient and dedicated in their
efforts to help him. Miss A., his new housemother, who has
remained a constant figure in his life, tried to accept his babyish
behaviour and carried him everywhere for months. But she was
frightened and disturbed when she found that Keith had set fire
to a collection of cuddly toys he had loved. His teacher too was
puzzled and worried by the relentless way in which Keith would
suddenly destroy any small piece of work they had been able to
do together. Despite daily personal attention from his class
teacher and remedial teacher he was unable to begin to learn to
read and remained in some profound sense untouchable.

When he could be controlled at school no longer he was referred
again to the clinic. The school had struggled on with him for three
years – a testimony, no doubt, to the good will and compassion of
the teachers, but perhaps also to something in Keith himself, some
quality which had inspired devotion in Miss A., which has kept
him coming to his psychotherapy sessions for nearly five years
with no absences due to anything other than illness.

Keith began once-weekly treatment when he was 9 years old. He
began coming twice weekly a year later, at his own request. Over
the years there have been many complex issues concerning the

management of the case, particularly in relation to the children's home, schools and the social services department. The extent and importance of this aspect of organising and maintaining support in order to make continuity of therapy possible is a dimension of the work with such children already stressed in Chapter 1. (See also Chapters 12 and 13.)

Keith was a small and delicately boned child, strikingly beautiful with honey-coloured skin and large, dark, serious eyes. He was unusually graceful and has always used his body to express himself most vividly. He has sometimes looked tiny and fragile, vulnerable to an extreme degree; at other times he has carried himself with a jaunty, cavalier manner conveying a kind of deft, quick cynicism. Keith has never talked very much in the sessions though later he was able to converse much more. But it took a long while for this kind of communication to develop. Keith's first concern was to know what was going to happen to him. The one and only time he ever used a ruler to draw straight lines was in his first session when he drew an orderly ship on a flat and waveless ocean. He was upset when some black got out of the ship and into the, as yet, unperturbed sea. I think he felt, and indeed it turned out to be true, that things inside him were going to start getting out and that he wouldn't know what they were and where they would go, or even if there would be anywhere they could go. That first drawing remained the only drawing of the year. This more organised and deliberate mode of expression quickly gave way to what was a much more authentic, though far less comprehensible way of showing what he was feeling. Keith just crashed everything – his toys, the furniture, himself. Throughout he would ask anxiously, 'How long have I got? How long have I got?' He did this in every session for well over a year. He seemed preoccupied with falling. When he started using his toys as distinct rather than indiscriminate pieces of equipment, he would drop cars and dolls from as high as he could get in the room, making below a scene of carnage with red paint carefully spattered to effect blood spurting from bodies. These scenes he would survey from several angles. He would jump from the window sill and the chest of drawers or stare down out of the window to the ground. Later he used to spit from as high as he could get and watch the blob of saliva fall and splatter.

In these and other ways I felt that Keith conveyed to me his anxiety about being dropped, about having no one and no way for his experience to be caught and held. I think he felt like his cars and dolls – crashed senselessly over and over again. And I think he was afraid that his therapy would be just like that. He told me about a bonfire where a boy fell in and got burned up – there was nothing left but his teeth. Keith would walk around tapping his teeth and shooting the occasional apprehensive glance at me.

However, he did have some dim idea of finding something for himself, but he didn't know what it could be. He asked me in his third session whether he would be getting orange juice. No amount of explanation or interpretation on my part could quench his thirst for the concrete gratifications he wanted from therapy and which he believed were available to other children in the building.

As Keith gradually came to recognise his sessions as a place to put his confused and fragmented fallings and crashes, and as he came to see me as someone who was interested in his state of mind, his communication became clearer; for instance, the pinched-off bits of plasticine he often left on the window sill became the bones on a skeleton island. There were several bodies and amongst them were two boys – one died and one escaped. The one who escaped came back two years later to see the bones of his friends. In such play, Keith seemed torn between allowing the birth of his phantasies and smashing their tentative beginnings. His play suggested some wish to know about his past and what had happened to him, but the pain which this aroused was more than he could bear and he would try to obliterate the meaning of his thoughts and feelings by attacking them in me. He would scream how stupid I was, what a mental place the clinic was, how dumb the sessions were. These early sessions were often overwhelmed by a raging senselessness which defied a belief in meaning as a healing experience. Nevertheless, Keith was able to go on to show me the bones and tell me what a 'desert' place the island was and how terrible.

I think that he was expressing in the story of the skeleton island what he felt was the dilemma with which his therapy faced him. If his inside world was littered with the parental figures he had never known and lost and those he had known and lost, how could he come and look at the deadness and the slaughter which preceded it? In a session following the 'skeleton island' session Keith came walking tall and 'snazzy', as he said. He kept telling me he was 'not getting stupid'. I felt he needed this snazzy, tough self to protect him from feeling stunned by the impact of his infantile feelings. Keith couldn't keep still, jumping all around the room and yelling over and over, 'How much time? How much time?' I asked him how much he felt he needed. Furious, he shouted, '200,000 years to destroy the world.'

One of the reasons that Keith felt his therapy would take so long was his deep conviction that I was concealing from him numerous other children more privileged than himself. As we approached the second holiday he began to hunt these other children. He would run suddenly from the room and race through the clinic darting from floor to floor while I called after him, 'Keith, your session is only in Room 8'. His favourite place was the canteen. Keith complained bitterly that his session room was on the first floor. He wanted it higher and believed that the other children got to have their sessions on the top floor. He inspected our room for the marks of other children and if by some stroke of misfortune one of the other children's drawers was left unlocked he would have it opened quick as a flash and pull out some ball or marble and, holding it over his head, say with indignant grievance, 'There, you see what they've got.'

Keith seemed to feel that he was the baby his mother threw away like some dirty piece of old rubbish – hence his lowly position on the first floor and his inferior toys. But more, he felt that she had

gone to other preferred children who got fed upstairs and received
wonderful toys. He conveyed to me his deep conviction that he was
not the kind of baby who could be fed at the breast and cherished.
I once made the mistake of wearing a locket in a session and before
I knew what was happening Keith had ripped it from my neck and
was desperately trying to open it to see 'the baby inside that you
love best'.

As time went by Keith found more and more ways of expressing
his feelings about the other children and about himself in relation
to them and me. He started calling the other children mongols,
mongrels and tiny mingrils. He said they were spastic and mental
and paki-bastards. During the second year of treatment he acquired
a swagger and a thick thug-like expression. He would roll into the
room and boast to me how he and the 'local lads' were going to kill
twenty paki-babies. His cruelty became increasingly delineated as
he mutilated his dolls, tortured them by squeezing them in the
window or hanging them upside down. Needless to say, Keith felt
tormented and invaded by the children he so hated. Towards the
end of a session particularly filled with contempt he said, 'Naughty
Neddy wants to go to an island in the Pacific, no the Atlantic,
about the size of the clinic with palm trees. He'll have lots to drink
and eat and colour telly. And he'll have monsters to keep the paki-
babies away from him.'

But Keith's cruelty was not only directed at the other children,
it was also meant to crush his own feelings of neediness and
vulnerability. A figure appeared, in gesture rather than words,
which had the soft, baby quality of a kitten. Keith thought he saw
what he called a 'pany-cat' outside the clinic. He would make some
funny little movement with his hand like a paw or wait for me in
the waiting room curled up on the sofa. This pany-cat Keith was
open to attack by the local lads and eventually succumbed to their
brutality in a most interesting way - that is, by joining in with the
mockery. What had originally been sincere portraits of smallness
became broad slapstick, caricatures of infantile states. Keith would
waddle towards me or talk in a mock baby-voice or even stand in
front of me drooling and blinking. I felt that not only was it Keith
playing the fool but also it was meant to make me feel like a fool for
ever taking seriously the longing of the child standing in front of
me.

I simply could not tell when he was being sincere. When I tried
to describe this to him once as me being like a mummy, so stupid
she could recognise neither her own baby nor the difference
between good and bad, Keith said sarcastically, 'You're quick.'
This in fact was quite the opposite of the truth, for this subtle
robbery had been going on for months under my very nose and
soon found its essential expression in some new characters which
emerged in Keith's play.

Before the third summer holiday Keith began to talk about a
rabbit named 'Rabino'. He would call out his name repeatedly,
playing with the vowel sounds - 'Ra, Ra, Ra, Beenoo, Beenoo
Bunny.' He would tell me coyly what Rabino ate, where he hopped,

how cute he was and how he liked to sleep with Keith. Keith
presented the rabbit as cute and cuddly, though from the beginning
I had my doubts. It was, he said, going to hide in my suitcase when
I went on holiday and pop out when I arrived at my destination. I
appreciated that Keith wanted to be inside me to avoid separation;
however, what I did not fully appreciate at the time was that he
intended to swap Rabino as a faecal facsimile of a baby for a real
baby he believed I would have during the holiday. In other words,
the intention was murder, but it was smeared over with a cloying
bunny disguise.

Rabino was prolific over the holiday: he had given birth to three
guinea pigs, known as ra-guineas to denote their origin. Now in
sessions Keith would make a grunting 'Ra-ra-ra' deep in his throat,
often following this by a visit to the toilet, during which he would
ask me for lots of loo paper and sing to himself, 'loo-poo, loo-poo,
ra-guinea, ra-guinea, ra-guinea'. He would come out of the toilet
heady with his production, grinning and flicking his tongue in and
out. He would tell me that Rabino had done lots of poos and talk
adoringly of the clever guineas.

Keith became obsessed with sewers. He wanted to know where all
the sewers in London were and questioned me endlessly about the
drainage system of the clinic. He wanted to go down in a sewer and
when I asked him what he wanted to do there, he said, 'Just stand
and look.'

As this material gathered momentum over the months I felt
increasingly helpless and overwhelmed, almost drowned in this
effluence of projections which seemed to have no end. The room was
awash with the sewage of phoney idealisations. Keith was not looking for a cleansing or clarifying maternal object: he needed a drain.

He invented three cats, Comfy, Toby and Erica (later known as
Buggin, when its true nature was revealed). At first these cats
seemed to have something of the pany-cat about them. He described them in realistic detail and spoke of them tenderly. But they
soon became grouped with Rabino and the guineas. All the animals
had anal intercourse with each other and Keith would gaily sing
'Willy-bum, willy-bum bum', and tell me how they licked their bums
and willies and made poo-babies. Keith kitted out these faecal
creatures with a large repertoire of noises, gestures and songs.
He also developed several different ways of hoiking up his mucus,
stretching and pulling it, and finally eating it in front of me. He
spat almost continuously, although rarely, I am happy to say,
directly at me. He relentlessly asserted the superiority of this life
in the sewer, for instance, telling me that I couldn't have one of
his delicious chips because I was not a poo-baby. It would seem
that Keith had to a large extent identified himself as a poo-baby,
the product of anal intercourse. He strove to exalt himself as
'Boogie King Baby', as the lyric of one of his songs said, independent of any mother figure for sustenance, because he had so many
poo-babies of his own, and unaware of time because, as he said,
'the session is a never ending poo.'

When I spoke to Keith about the fact that one day he would stop therapy, he flatly denied this. When I said that all babies one day did stop sucking their mother's breasts or bottle, he turned on me in fury, kicking and hitting me. 'Nobody has to stop anything,' he said. When I said that although he wished this was true it was not, he replied, 'Well, I don't have to stop.'

As we came to the end of Keith's fourth year of therapy, I felt little optimism as to the prospect of Keith's willingness to relinquish his own bottom as a replacement for the breast he knew he must lose in the external world. The possibility of internalising a sound maternal object seemed constantly undermined by the fear and the feeling that no mother could possibly survive the deluge of dirt and destruction. The false promises of Keith's anal world were hard to resist. At least with Rabino he need never ask, 'How long have I got?'

I would like to restate or underline aspects of Keith's treatment which I feel have particular relevance to his experience of abandonment and early deprivation.

The first is chaos, the dread of falling to pieces or being burned up by nameless feelings. I think that abandonment has meant to Keith being flung violently into a senseless whirlwind of sensation and feeling. Gradually in the sessions he has developed a hope and expectation that his experiences are meaningful and can be understood.

In the session just before his first holiday, Keith cried and moaned, 'I want a boat, I want a boat! Why don't you give me a boat?' He was inconsolable and made me know the sickening unpredictability of his babyhood and how desperately he longed for something concrete to hold and protect him from the waves of panic with which every change and loss threatened him.

How can our words begin to correspond properly to the sensations of infantile experience? Sometimes it seemed as though it was the sound of my voice that carried and held him and if I stopped it meant I put him down.

This emphasis on sensation and the physical beginnings of mental experience is something which I feel may be particularly poignant in the treatment of deprived children. The visceral dimension of the counter-transference seems important and useful as part of the understanding of the patient. When I accompanied Keith along the corridor I often felt like a mother duck fluffing out her feathers to shelter her baby, and if I failed to mentally cover him in this peculiar way he was likely to make inappropriate dashes at things and people.

The gradual conversion of such physical sensations into imagery and finally into meaningful thoughts seems to me especially important for these children who have not had the normal experiences which are necessary for any baby to learn to think.

The second aspect of Keith's therapy which I think reflects what his experience of repeated primary loss has become inside him is the preoccupation with cruelty which became so dominant in his second year of treatment. In part this cruelty was retributive. I was seen as a rich mother tormenting Keith with therapy, showing this hungry baby the breast and then taking it away to give it to my real babies. The other children – the mongols, spastics and paki-bastards – were made to suffer in Keith's play the degradation, humiliation and pain he felt had been deliberately inflicted upon him. I, as the tantalising maternal figure, have had my hopes for his growth and development repeatedly and cruelly crushed.

I think that Keith's preoccupation with cruelty has also been a kind of highly charged, immediate antidote to depression. The sharp excitement of torture has seemed to momentarily blast him away from pity and despair. He has used it to detonate his feelings of loss and sorrow but this, of course, has also left him feeling ill and afraid he will not be able to grow up and that he will, as he has said, go to jail when he is 16½ years old.

As his fears about growing began to come more and more into his therapy there came with this also some hopefulness about the future. He has touched me deeply by his passionate and violent struggle to survive the disaster of his infancy.

5 SEXUALITY AND AGGRESSION AS RELATED THEMES

Rolene Szur

Certain common features emerging during the therapy of a number of children in care have suggested that it would be helpful to direct attention to the appearance of markedly precocious or perverse sexuality as a significant feature of a child's relationships and activities. This may express a frustrated longing for closeness and affection, or perversely may serve to belittle and denigrate relationships, turning instead to sensual excitement for relief from loneliness and anxiety. In these ways it can be recognised as a precursor of the disturbances of sexuality which have been more commonly studied as manifestations of adult emotional life. The sexualisation of interactions between children and adults imposes a fictitious peer-relationship that essentially denies or distorts the child's need to depend on adults for care and protection.

The denigrating elements are more clearly evident when there is an association with delinquent or aggressive forms of acting out, although any overt sexual behaviour is generally difficult to tolerate in children's homes and similarly disturbing to adoptive or foster-families. Chris, the little girl in Chapter 3 who had been rejected by her mother, stole and exhibited herself. She seemed to be trying at the age of 11 to act out confused phantasies of herself as a meretricious mother with a baby of her own, in order to avoid the bitterness of her rejection and the fear of its repetition. The defensive uses of sexualisation can also become apparent in the therapeutic setting, and 10 year old Desmond, described later in this chapter, showed this clearly. When, for example, he was facing the anxieties of a number of changes in his life, including the risk of a separation from his therapist, he contrived to establish a flirtatious and flaunting relationship with another adult, thus setting up rifts and antagonisms between a number of parental figures.

During the last two decades it has become evident that physical abuse of children is more widespread than had previously been recognised (Creighton, 1979). Recent studies indicate that this is true also of the sexual seduction or exploitation of children (Mrazek and Kempe; 1981; Bentovim et al., 1981) whether of a voyeuristic or exhibitionistic nature, or through more direct involvement. A child's vulnerability to sexual exploitation by adults may stem from the presence of a longing at conscious and unconscious levels to be loved by mother or father (Freud, 1909), however confused the accompanying phantasies may be. A tubby 11-year-old girl of normal intelligence involved with a friend of her father's in posing for quite alarming pornographic pictures, was presented by him

with the gift of a doll and perambulator. When referred for therapy
she conveyed an incongruous impression, as if she were in identification with some image of a seductive fecund mother who had taken
the sexuality and babies away from some discarded drudge mother.
Relationships with her own mother and with her peers were very
poor.

For the reasons referred to above, rejected or neglected children
could therefore form an especially vulnerable group. A precocious
or pathological sexualisation of childhood relationships, whatever
the precipitating factors may have been, is likely to affect and
distort not only personal relationships but development in other
fields also.

On a purely behavioural level it has been suggested (Shengold,
1967) that children who have suffered 'experiences involving overstimulation', including being beaten often and severely, or being
exposed repeatedly to observation of intercourse, or sexually
seduced, were later driven to violent acting out. This was seen as
a repetitive attempt to attain some discharge for the excessive
excitation, or to find relief for rages of an overwhelming infantile
intensity. One may wonder whether the repetitive violent activities
of children such as Tom in Chapter 4 or Desmond have some of this
quality. In terms of psychological damage Hyatt Williams (1976)
has found that the factor of helplessness in the face of violence
or violent scenes increases the effect of long-term disturbance. It
may be that overwhelming submission to others could be shattering
to the sense of personal identity.

It was noted that in a number of the deprived children referred
for treatment, aggressiveness and delinquency were associated with
sadistic sexualised elements, together in some cases with a considerable preoccupation with anality. It may be that for these groups of
children the association between sexuality and hostility may have
specific roots in a feeling that the absent mothers and fathers
represent a sexuality totally divorced from good parenting functions.
Their children could therefore feel themselves to be either the
victims or the waste-products of a degraded intercourse, rather
than the progeny of any creative relationship.

In so far as the therapist might represent externally the image of
a good and concerned parent, the child may feel a compulsive need
to deny and to destroy the pain of longing for this kind of relationship. This would lead to an attack on aspects of therapy which the
patient experienced as being in touch with these lonely areas of
his inner world.

Sometimes a patient, like for example Keith, described in the
previous chapter, reveals a specifically disturbing quality of cruelty,
while Tom perhaps finds that he cannot start to be forgiving until
he has managed somehow to 'even up the scores' in suffering since
in his own early history the scales have been just too heavily loaded
against him. There are also grounds for believing that he may have
been subject to a degree of physical abuse before coming into care.
At one time when children were found to be suffering from ill-
treatment the main work was directed towards promoting change in

the adults concerned (or removing them). It is now increasingly recognised that even when the parents have been helped to the point where physical injury is 'dramatically reduced' or ceases, the degree of disturbance suffered by the children remains extremely high (Trowell and Castle, 1981, see also Kempe, 1978, Giaretto, 1981).

While recognising that there could be specific factors for the kinds of difficulties which are being discussed, it is necessary to recall that these disturbances are not limited to children (or adults) with histories of deprivation and trauma. We should therefore consider the nature of perversion as a general phenomenon. While giving full attention to individual ways of responding to personal experiences, it may be especially important, when working with children who are in care, fostered, or adopted, to keep in mind that their experiences and phantasy lives are also variations on universal themes, in the context of human growth and development.

From the beginning of life physiological growth and functioning can be seen as interrelating with the growth of personality, sensory and sensual experience with infantile 'pre-genital' sexuality (Freud, 1905a), and all linking in many complex ways with the development of character traits and personal relationships. Thus infants' earliest sensual experiences of sucking and biting can be correlated with shifts from states in which there may be only a little sense of separateness from mother or states of contented dependency, to times of frustration, loneliness and fear, which could be experienced as resentful, hostile neediness. At this time the baby is a very dependent creature and the relationship with the mother may be strongly coloured by images of her as the loving provider - or depriving non-provider - of a feeding breast, a warm lap and a dry napkin, but not yet fully apprehended as another or a whole personality.

At the same time an increasing control of bowel and bladder may bring the infant a growing sense of physical and personal control and prowess. Sometimes this can be seen to be allied to destructive and rejecting feelings. (Tom's use of obscene language and his soiling and wetting provide vivid illustrations of the way in which the evacuation and projection of unwanted feelings can seem to be the psychological equivalent of the processes of defaecating or urinating, in a manner which relieves the child but despoils the mother and her image.) But of course at other times achievement of such physiological controls can be felt as good and satisfying both to babies themselves and to the objects of their closest attachment, generally mother and father in the first instance. (One can see evidence of this in Tom's later efforts to clean up his conversation, and his wish to 'train'.)

As a mother comes to be valued increasingly for herself as a whole personality and less as a composite of parts to provide for varied needs, this may lead on to the emergence of love and concern for her as an individual, and similarly for father, and then brothers and sisters, in a gradually widening social circle. This struggle from early 'part object' relationships towards acknowledging the independent individual lives of others is complex and difficult and possibly never fully achieved by anyone. The severely disturbed children described in the previous chapter seem to suggest the image of an enraged baby who feels that when his parents are not instantly available to attend to his needs for food or evacuation, it is because they are attending to their own rival needs for sexual intercourse, envisaged simply as equivalent processes of feeding and evacuation.

Real ordinarily good or bad parents might sometimes seem to be hateful and hated, but at other times loving and loved, while continuing to survive as their individual selves, holding together both good and bad experiences in a more balanced way. Parent figures secretly damaged or destroyed in phantasy often seem to represent the greatest fears. They combine the danger of retaliation for children's imagined attacks, with the threat of drawing them towards the threshold of guilt and anxiety, and so need to be destroyed over and over again. In some cases these frightening aspects of the parental figures may be denied and projected instead into outside impersonal agencies, the social services or the law. Complex internal dramas which reflect these patterns can be seen in the descriptions of Desmond's sessions later in this chapter. Sometimes, for example, he struggles to project frightening figures into the therapist, and sometimes to force him into carrying the role of the victim, processes which can be described as invasive or 'projective identification' (Klein, 1946). This illustrates also how similar patterns are carried on in physically and sexually abusive families, with hatred and guilt passing back and forth, and the fear of accepting outside help. The children may be trapped at conscious and unconscious levels by conflicting needs and loyalties as well as through their physical helplessness.

'Identification with the aggressor', as defined by Anna Freud (1937, p. 118), represents a way of mastering fear of a 'dreaded external object' by assimilating or identifying with it. This could be linked not only with aggressiveness but also with the deeply confused sense of identity and of values, which is often so self-destructive. (The short story In the Penal Settlement by Franz Kafka (1933) offers a vivid literary presentation of this state of mind.)

A child's phantasy of a good and creative parental relationship seems to be fundamental to his or her image of all healthy relationships, representing a bringing together of what are considered to be masculine and feminine sides of the personality, an alliance or friendship, and a benign sexuality. If the child's phantasies are distorted by jealousy, envy or distressing experiences, this may lay the foundation for the perverse sexuality defined by Stoller (1976) as 'the erotic form of hatred'.

In discussing distinctions between infantile or childhood sexuality and adult sexuality, Meltzer (1973) outlines a formulation which emphasises motivation. Whereas infantile sexuality is characterised as being experimental and imitative in terms of phantasies about the parental relationship, and predominantly masturbatory in aim, adult sexuality is envisaged as essentially creative and reciprocal.

Similarly, what constitutes the element of perversion in sexuality is
a perverseness of aim, destructiveness in motivation, and unconscious phantasies in which bad parts of the self bring confusion
and destruction to the image of the creative couple and their
creativity. This implies also an attack on the other babies who are
created, that is on the aspect of the intercourse as productive work.
In this connection it is interesting to notice that as Tom's relationship to his therapist begins to improve, his capacity to work also
comes to life (Chapter 4). In clinical work with children and adolescents it is necessary therefore to distinguish between simple
precocity and perversion. The most striking feature which one
experiences in personal encounters with children under the sway of
perverse images could be dramatically stated in the words of the
witch in Shakespeare's 'Macbeth' who cries,

> Fair is foul and foul is fair,
> Hover through the fog and filthy air.

At a primitive level of experience sadistic anal perversions appear
to manifest unconscious phantasies which idealise the infantile
world of part objects, denying reality and destroying all distinctions
between good and bad, between parents and children or between
the sexes, as if all may be reduced to the level of fodder or faeces
(Chasseguet-Smirgel, 1978; Meltzer, 1973). Images of women and
men as sex objects belong to similar levels of experience. There is
considerable evidence of these qualities in some of the drawings
and stories produced by Desmond, and in the following pages
aspects of his problems and development are described by his
therapist (a man).

Desmond
Desmond was referred for psychotherapy by the children's home at
the age of 10 when his vicious attacks on children at school and his
serious failure to achieve up to the standard of an above average
intelligence had led to a recommendation for transfer to a school for
maladjusted children. He then began attending for psychotherapy
three times a week and has continued for some four years.
    During this time he has shown a preoccupation with one central
theme in his life, which he calls 'the end'! Sometimes this seems to
refer to the separation from his family at the age of 7 when he first
went into care, but judging from the family history and from the
experience of therapy, an internal catastrophic experience of
separation must have taken place far earlier, and been repeated
many times before that final break.
    In the early weeks of therapy Desmond seemed to be anticipating
'the end' in some form of violent expulsion, and subsequently again
and again set up situations which threatened to precipitate just
such an ending. This phrase, as he uses it, has a fatalistic ring
of utter finality, which conveys Desmond's disbelief in a life-giving
concern for him on the part of another person; it conveys also
the tantalising quality of much of his material in which the prevailing

sense of dread and persecution has been tinged with a sense of sadness and longing.

The main forms of his communications have been through his drawings which convey in stark form the picture he seems to carry within himself of a relationship in which the qualities are essentially those of persecutor and victim. These too are the roles which have passed endlessly to and fro in a prolonged struggle between patient and therapist. From an early date he made drawings of me with a dripping nose, which together with other material, conjured up a picture of a tearful sniffing red-eyed mother who eternally dripped her own excessive depression or illness on to the baby lying in her lap. In terms of the transference relationship this suggested that Desmond saw me as a maternal figure that would be incapable of absorbing and holding on to any of his own infantile pain and unwanted feelings. On the contrary he seemed to perceive me as consistently projecting into him aspects of myself that I could not contain.

Such a relationship between mother and baby could have contributed to his frequently experiencing anything I said as attacking, equated with mucus or faeces, and he reciprocated by literally hawking up and spitting out phlegm at me. At one time, at the height of what had developed into a vicious circle, there was an excited, sensual quality in such behaviour, as if in Desmond's unconscious phantasy the exchange of my words and his phlegm represented some form of perverse and sadistic intercourse. During this same period of time he was also developing a seductive, exhibitionistic relationship with an adult in the environment, through which he attempted to make either myself or the young man carry the role of the child, excluded from the exciting parental relationships, though compelled to be an onlooker. The enactment of such scenes by Desmond may well have reflected events in his earlier life when he is known to have been present during some alcoholic and promiscuous escapades. Many of his drawings suggest that he witnessed excesses of this kind. One of these depicted a family engaged in an oral, anal and genital orgy, which he described as the therapist's family Christmas dinner.

Another was a portrait of the therapist composed entirely of penises for limbs head and trunk. It was clear that he identified himself with this as a destructive male genital in his efforts to denigrate, humiliate, and to wreak havoc in the room and destroy the therapy. Sometimes it did not seem to be aimed so much at the therapist in a personal way as at the total experience of therapy as an attempt to find meaning. When this was happening he seemed primarily engaged in attacking my capacity to think, perhaps as representing a parental capacity for creativity at any level.

At a later date, when he was more in touch with the consequences of his destructiveness, Desmond dreamed of a 'sand monster', first referred to by a slip of the tongue as a 'sad monster'. This creature was constantly being felled by stones thrown by Desmond, but still rose up to chase him, despite the fact that the stones 'had made a hole in his head.' I thought that this creature in the dream represented myself, and perhaps was also a reflection of his mother's sad or depressed state linked with me in the transference (see Figure 5.1).

Figure 5.1

Sometimes Desmond seemed to be identified with some boss figure, representing someone who ran the clinic and me. At these times he seemed less crudely bullying but more coldly impersonal in his violence. This absent but strongly felt persecutor (he never knew his real father) was vividly implied in drawings of machines that dealt out torture and death. A victim would be tied down and watching with tears the approach of a circular saw, axes, or a pendulum, or some such instrument, while the complex machinery that worked these instruments apparently lacked a human operator. In one drawing of a torture dungeon the 'boss' or 'Tavvi Governor', as he was sometimes called, was upstairs out of sight but able to hear the cries and screams (Figure 5.2)

These images corresponded very closely with the feeling Desmond conveyed of a cold impersonal and inexorable decision-making apparatus that would end his therapy as cruelly and peremptorily as he had evidently felt himself cut off in the past. Needless to say, the situation was reversed so that I was meant to feel the victim of this process. At times when he was able to attack me less and be more in touch with the sadness and sense of loss that lay beneath the rage, Desmond would feel the torment all the more keenly - and so would I - for what I was torturing him with then was the communication of sadness.

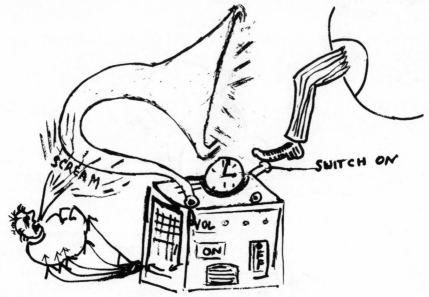

Figure 5.2

We swung therefore from states of feeling persecuted to experiencing considerable depression and then back again, to a state in which all his neediness and vulnerability could be located in me, and there be attacked and got rid of. As I have said, the roles of victim and aggressor interchanged constantly between us. One consequence of his barrage of violence and obscene images was that I found it hard to avoid enacting the qualities of the persecutor. Sometimes I was precipitated into action that was, in retrospect, premature and which played into the picture of sadist and tormentor which he made of me. At times I was driven to make interpretations as much in self-defence as in order to shed light, and to think aloud as a way of holding my own mental processes in some order - in either case tormenting him.

At one time I felt myself under pressure to end therapy altogether, and I began to understand how workers involved with children such as Desmond can be driven to act precipitately or harshly despite their best intentions, and ultimately to get rid of them.

On the other side of the coin, as persecutor rather than victim, Desmond did his best to defame me, expose me as a molestor and pervert or else as an inadequate therapist who could do nothing to control him or protect him from the consequences of his aggression. I was the one who would then have to pay the price, both emotionally and financially, for the destruction of the room, and answer for the perverse acts that he accused me of, at the top of his voice. This would, he phantasised, lead to my dismissal rather than his, but either way round 'the end' would have been brought about yet again. The compulsion to bring about a repetition of the original catastrophe seemed to fulfil at least two functions. He would both end the anguish of anticipation which was central to the torture, and also bring the torture and the end under his own control.

Figure 5.3

The picture I have so far given of Desmond applies in this extreme way to a period covering the first fifteen months of therapy. Subsequently, under conditions of stress, such as at times when decisions have had to be made about schooling and whether he

should move to a home for older children, or at the time when his
mother was pregnant, the state of mind and behaviour described
has reasserted itself, though in a progressively attenuated form.

His aggression seems to have been contained in therapy to the
extent that he has held his place quite successfully in his secondary school. Lately, coming up to the end of the fourth year in
treatment, he has shown clear evidence of being able to discuss
plans - breaks, holiday dates, school trips, and even fostering,
in advance, and for example has been giving me notice when he
expects to be unable to attend. In the context of Desmond's
psychopathology these are, for him, crucial issues. This seems to
indicate that he has begun to internalise a figure that treats him
with concern and to whom he can in turn show consideration. It also
gives some cause to hope that 'the end', like the breaks in therapy,
each one an end in itself, is not the attacking thing that it once
was. At the end of his second year, before the long summer holiday,
Desmond drew a picture of a road with a gap in it. Below the gap
was water and the open jaws of a monstrous object waiting for the
figure above to fall through the gap. The latter was meanwhile
leaping as if nonchalant and unaware across the gap on roller
skates. (Figure 5.3)

Desmond is now faced with the end of therapy on a three-times-
a-week basis, and also with the possibility of being fostered,
which would mean leaving the children's home that has held on to
him, through thick and thin, for the past six years.

Therapy is denigrated now in proportion to the extent to which a
future foster-family is idealised. There are signs that puberty is
making him think about the nature of his sexuality and the kind of
offspring that such a sexuality might produce. The last few months
of intensive therapy will be important in helping him decide whether
he himself is the 'waste product of a bad intercourse' and as such
experiencing rejection and expulsion by me; or whether he can feel
himself to be a legitimate offspring with a right to a place of his
own in the world.

In thinking about work with children who have suffered deprivation
or inadequate parenting, and who are preoccupied with violence,
it seems relevant to draw attention to the considerable risk that they
may later become parents who can deal with inner stress only through
projecting suffering and guilt into those around them, or achieve
some relief by externalising conflicts. (Fraiberg, 1980; Steele and
Alexander, 1981). Situations of this kind sometimes arise for the
parents of babies who are born sick or premature requiring some
period of hospitalisation, like Katy in Chapter 3.

The incidence of ill-treatment in this group is disproportionately
high. (Bentovim, 1977, Hunter et al., 1978; Lynch et al., 1975).
This seems to be due in part to feelings that the baby's illness
represents an accusation, and a rejection of the parents as not good
enough. An image of the baby as hostile can hinder the development
of attachment. Where parents' own experiences have been very harsh
they may have especial difficulty in keeping in touch with their

capacities for being accepting and caring, being very quickly provoked into feeling angry and rejected by any childish complaints or challenges.

In treating deprived children we are often aware, therefore, of being in touch with part of a cycle in the transmission of pain and confusion across the generations. External events have brought them more than ordinary distress, and the work of relieving the good and hopeful parts of their personalities from the tyranny of the cynical and bad can be an especially long and hard task for patient, therapist and residential workers.

6 TECHNICAL PROBLEMS IN THERAPY

Mary Boston

Many of these severely disturbed children present particular problems of technique and management in the course of psychotherapy. Tom, Keith and Desmond showed aggression and cruelty which was difficult to control and to contain. All the children, at times, some in more subtle ways than others, made their therapists feel useless, helpless, rejected, abandoned, messed up or cruelly treated – precisely the experiences and feelings which the patients themselves found intolerable or hard to bear.

This reversal of the painful experience seems very important in trying to understand children who do not find it easy to communicate in words. Their behaviour itself is often the vital message. It is our task to receive and respond appropriately. We may have little to go on apart from the feelings we experience ourselves.

Susie, a little girl of 4, who had been taken into care by the police very abruptly, in the middle of the night, because of sexual abuse by her father, was cutting out a pattern in a piece of paper. Her therapist described the scene thus:

> Susie assumes the air of an authoritative adult. 'Now you fold it like this, right? And then like this, right? Right! Then that' (very cross because of lack of expected response from the therapist). She opens up the paper and draws some small dots. There is vicious hard cutting with pieces falling on to the floor. The impression is as if something marvellous is going to emerge. Meanwhile she is singing 'See saw, Jenny shall have a new master'. This is related by the therapist to the sudden changes she has experienced, her feelings perhaps not having been taken into account. Susie continues, 'There goes a sister. Like this, right? There goes an arm. Cut that leg off. I like cutting people's arms and legs and heads. Oh yes, and now do you see what we've got? (unfolding) 'It's a . . . (trumpet sound) bloody mess.' The therapist is trying not to cry. There is a heavy, infinitely sad pause.

In this scene Susie seems to be trying to deal with her feelings of being cut into pieces by the abrupt removal from home and parents by becoming the cruel cutter up herself, at the same time poignantly mocking the no doubt well-meaning intentions of the adults concerned. The pain and sadness are experienced by the therapist.

Desmond's machine (see Figure 5.2) illustrates in a similarly vivid way the torture he experienced in being kept in suspense regarding plans which might interfere with the continuation of therapy. However, very often this feeling was communicated to the therapist by enaction in which the therapist became the victim, the recipient of the boot, the spit and the 'fuck offs'.

Such aggressive and violent behaviour in therapy could be considered partly as revenge for rejection and abandonment, but it often also needed to be understood as the aggression of which the patient felt the recipient, rather than the perpetrator. This process makes interpretation tricky. Drawing attention to the child's overt aggression when he feels basically identified with the victim may be felt as adding insult to injury, as an unjust accusation.

It is probably technically very important to try to elucidate in detail the kinds of relationship which are being enacted, while being prepared, for a time, to accept the role of whatever figure the patient seems to need to project at that particular moment. It might be the victim or it might be the persecutor, the representative of the cruel system or the abandoning parent. In the latter cases the patient may attack in fear and self-defence. Alternatively he may deal with his fear in a counterphobic way, by getting into the shoes of the persecutor. 'If you can't beat 'em, join 'em.' The therapist may then be terrorised, representing the frightened or needy part of the patient.

A further complication is introduced when an internal configuration which Donald Meltzer (1973, p. 105) has called 'submission to tyranny' exists. This is where the patient feels enslaved by a part of the self which seems to offer a spurious protection against terror. It is like joining a gang or a protection racket in order not to get bullied (or, as with Keith, becoming a thug to hunt down the 'paki-babies'). There can then be a turning away from the truth and from a genuine dependence on the protection of a helpful parental figure from whom a source of real courage can be derived. The frightened needy aspects of the self then have to submit to the pseudo protection of the tyrant figure instead. When this internal situation, in the patient's mind, is enacted in the therapeutic relationship (and very often by general behaviour as well), the patient may play the role of the tyrant and the therapist (or other worker) might represent either the persecutor, against whom the tyrant promises protection, or the frightened part of the self. This kind of process is particularly likely to happen with deprived children whose experience of actual good parenting has been lacking.

The degree to which the patient is the slave to a cruel destructive part of his personality, addicted to a perverse, sado-masochistic enactment of such an internal constellation, seems to be important for the prognosis. It seems important, though not always easy, to differentiate between the kind of aggression and toughness which some of the patients use like armour to protect themselves against painful feelings and the more permanent and cynical turning away from dependence on any external figures. Ronald Britton (1978) suggests that the prognosis is better 'when a strong sense of injustice or deprivation is retained together with a sense of outrage or loss, and less hopeful when it has given way to a cynical disbelief in any real goodness.'

There are one or two children in the sample whose perverse
assertion of the superiority of their own mucus and faeces leads
one to despair about the possibility of ever achieving any genuine
dependence on a source of sustenance which is not part of the self.
In Keith, for example, we see a rather precarious balance between
cynicism and some belief in a good parenting relationship of which
he has been deprived. With Desmond there were times when he
seemed immovably in the grip of a cruel and destructive figure with
whom he was identified. Any more tender, loving aspects were
violently extruded or caricatured and mocked. Yet both these boys
made considerable improvements in their lives outside the therapy.
    Rosenfeld (1979), in talking of a group of borderline patients
who have suffered 'severe mental trauma in early infancy for long
periods', talks of the situation when the analyst's image becomes
fused or confused with the omnipotent self of the patient. Any
interpretation of projection may be thrown back at the analyst (with
our child patients often literally thrown or spat). Rosenfeld suggests
(p. 206),

giving the patient time to get over the confusion, by allowing him
to express his anger, observations and criticisms, without attempting more than tentative infrequent interpretative work. This means
that it is analytically essential to assist the patient to bring his
often completely distorted image of the analyst right into the open,
which helps the patient to experience the analyst as a receptive
and accepting person who can contain the patient's projection.
Too immediate an interpretation of projection often has the opposite
effect, namely the creation of a rejecting image of the analyst.

In our experience with deprived children, such premature interpretation can be felt as further aggression against the patient and
so prolong or escalate the vicious circle of attack and defence which
is going on both externally and internally.
    When physical violence is a problem, limits may need to be set,
even to the extent of stopping sessions in some cases, until the
patient can regain control. It seems important to 'survive' with
children whose inner parental figures may be felt to be so fragile
and inadequate.
    Unsatisfactory early experiences, of violence, abuse and neglect,
unmodified by loving and supportive reality experiences, may leave
residual memories and feelings which are difficult to assimilate and
digest. These may constitute intrapsychic configurations which are
liable to be triggered off and re-enacted when an external situation
seems to match the early memory. This process has been described
by Hyatt Williams (1980) in his studies of murderers. It throws
light on the tendency for the early tragedies to repeat themselves,
for the abandoned child to become the abandoning parent and for
the cycle of deprivation to be perpetuated.
    It is essential for the therapist to resist being drawn into this
vicious circle, and to endure the emotional impact of these onslaughts

while setting firm limits to the physical expression of them 'as far as humanly possible. The temptation to give up and abandon the patient is often strong. 'Sticking it out' in these difficult phases is very important if steady progress is to be made. The therapist has to be prepared to accept the degree of pain projected and to resist the pull to react to the hostility in a retaliatory or defensive way. It seems crucial for the therapist to establish himself or herself as a trustworthy, understanding and enduring person, so that the development of more trusting and concerned relationships can proceed. We see a glimpse of this eventually with Tom and many of the others.

HARD TO HOLD

A particularly difficult problem arises when the reversal mechanism manifests itself in a big way right at the beginning, so that the patient is very hard to engage or takes flight before he has really begun. The gap between the first and second session may be immediately experienced as a rejection and disillusionment of some idealised expectations. This was so with Bobby (Chapter 1). He became hostile and abusive at the second contact, dealing with his own feeling of disappointment by rejecting the therapist. This commonly observed reaction to early sessions may manifest itself in a variety of ways, directly or indirectly. There may be overt abuse, the 'fuck off', as with Bobby, or more subtle expressions of it, not turning up to the next session, for example. Mistakes and confusions over appointments are frequently enactments of feelings of being unwanted which are unconsciously thrown back to the therapist. It is the therapist who is left, abandoned, not knowing if the client will come. This difficulty can make it very hard to know in advance what frequency of treatment would be most appropriate. For some children like Bobby once-weekly sessions seem to impose an intolerable gap from one week to the next in which they experience anew their feelings of being let down. Ruth, an adolescent who had herself asked for help, seemed to find it very difficult to get going at the beginning of every session. Her favourite expressions were 'I'm not bothered' and 'not really'. She professed no problems yet usually began to warm up as the session drew to a close, forcing her therapist to interrupt her when the time was up. The therapist felt very bad, as if she were pushing her out, and, as likely as not, Ruth would not appear next time, and when she did, the process of the slow warming-up would be repeated. The therapist felt that more frequent sessions might have engaged her more satisfactorily and prevented her from breaking off after a few months' treatment. Her children's home did report an improvement in her behaviour, but it was felt that she would have benefited by longer attendance.

In contrast, other children can make use of once-weekly help, even if they seem unreachable and show the brick wall kind of defence, as with Martin (Chapter 1). Some seem more threatened by frequent sessions, as if afraid of being touched or of depending on a therapist who will inevitably abandon them. Richard (Chapter 15), who broke off therapy in an angry and rejecting way, after only a few sessions, did seem to feel in danger of being touched emotionally. There was a good deal of confusion about times of appointments at the beginning which may have accentuated his feeling of being unwelcome. It was open to speculation whether more frequent sessions from the beginning would have 'held' him better, or led to flight even earlier. The actual breaking off came after the first holiday interval which for all the patients is a critical time. The reaction to the first longish absence of the therapist arouses earlier experience of loss and each patient reacts in his or her individual way. The terrors of such gaps in continuity are vividly illustrated in Desmond's gap drawing (see Figure 5.3). The therapist's work which is done repeatedly on the comings and goings in the treatment is very crucial in helping the patients to come to terms with their early separations.

In spite of initial difficulties in getting psychotherapy established, very few of the children actually broke off prematurely. Most became engaged in the work and the enactment of desertion took place within therapy, often freeing the patients to react in a more positive and less rejecting way to houseparents or foster-parents.

Two of the children who did terminate their sessions before the therapist thought they were ready (Valerie and Leroy) illustrate a further technical problem, withdrawal and silence. Again the therapist can feel very shut out, literally experiencing the rejection. Some dedication is needed to persevere in the face of apparent lack of response, as illustrated by Valerie's therapist.

Valerie
Valerie attended for therapy twice and then three times weekly for six months, when she was 14 years old.

Apart from some information dragged or coaxed from her in the initial interviews, she did not speak at all. She drew on two occasions after about a month of attendance, but otherwise sat silently in her chair. Mostly her silences, moods, facial expressions or hand movements seemed to be expressive and it was quite possible to try to understand something of their meaning, but sometimes I felt quite shut out and unable to work.

Valerie drew two caricature figures; a fat, complacent pig staring like a 'stupid judge', and, on the reverse of the page, a figure she called Timothy Winter 'with eyes and nails like splinters'. I under- stood the first as showing how she thought of me, and the second as revealing the sharp, attacking part of herself, that saw me in this way. These pictures seemed to characterise a number of her more hostile and suspicious sessions. However another drawing showed 'The Lady of Peace' whom she hoped would come to her. This was an idealised but quite sensitive drawing copied from a card which an old friend of her mother's had sent for her birthday. Having shown me these pictures it seemed that Valerie felt that she had said all that she could say or needed to say.

She was often in tears for short periods of her session; quite
often tears would trickle down from one eye only. The crying
seemed to be in response especially to interpretations about her
loneliness, her longing for a lost 'Lady of Peace' mother, her
withdrawal from the 'piggish', persecuting mothers in her present
life and in the session, and her seeking for a union with a lost
mother, but which led to her becoming identified with a dead or
depressed mother. Later, arising from reactions to holidays, it was
more possible to interpret her angry and bitterly hurt feelings that
her mother had not stayed alive for her sake; this produced
particularly sharp and painful reactions and was perhaps a central
factor in her depression.

Sometimes one hand would cradle and comfort the other but very
often she would dig her nails into the hand, back and fingers, and
pick and scratch and squeeze in a very attacking, painful way.
She either had or created an eczema-like condition on her hands,
and for long periods could be entirely lost and absorbed in these
cruel attacks. Later on there was some conscious attempt to restrain
hand-picking and some tender concern for the sore spots. I felt
these hand movements symbolised Valerie's attacks on her inner
image of a callous, indifferent mother and her seeking for some
comfort and concern. It may be that her hands were expressing the
unconscious phantasies in which she was absorbed, and represented
a relationship between a mother and her infant, who sometimes felt
cradled and comforted and at other times hurt and wounded.

Very often, however, there were long spells of passive withdrawal, gazing out of the window or into space, occasionally with
a little mouthing and tongue-sucking, making no indication of
response to anything I said. Eye contact was always avoided. My
vivid impression was that she was like a very passive baby who had
given up crying and the expectation that there was anyone to
respond to the crying, and who 'accepted' being dumped in the
pram or cot, giving no trouble, making no demands, but also rejecting any available contact, withdrawn into a phantasy of merging
with some permanently present maternal figure.

A number of situations such as, for example, changing appoint-
ment times for school examinations, her abortive first decision to
break off therapy, and similarly her choice of clothing, all revealed
how her apathy led her to accept a degree of institutionalisation, of
being treated as if she were a parcel to be sent here and there with
no say or choice for herself.

Physically she was mature for her age but initially showed no
sign of mental adolescence. This gradually emerged and strengthened. Her clothing became less like that of someone in mourning or
who wishes to pass unseen like a shadowy ghost, and more like that
of someone who has some sense of identity and attempts to declare
it - although she still remained unable to speak for herself. These
changes were accompanied by an increase of a more 'normal'
resistance to the elements of dependency which are intrinsic to the
treatment situation. There was an increase of stubbornness and
slightly more open hostility.

The final ending of treatment on her part may have been to some
degree a trying out of standing on her own feet, and prompted by
reaction to a holiday break - perhaps clutching at a straw of a
slight increase of strength for fear of drowning in the ocean of
painful feelings which remained hardly explored.

When treatment ended Valerie seemed slightly improved, and was
participating more in activities in the home and in school life. However, the seriousness of her states of withdrawal, depression and
social isolation remained a cause for considerable concern for her
mental health and stability. She and her housemother knew that she
could return to the clinic for consultation or help if required at any
future date.

A rather different picture was presented by Leroy. His withdrawal
had a flavour of explosiveness rather than apathy.

Leroy
Leroy, an 11-year-old boy, had been in care since he was three
weeks old. Though he came into care so early, it took more than
two years before it was certain that his future would not be with
his family. He was in a residential nursery until he was 5, in a
family group home until he was 10, and in an adolescent unit since
then. During this time there had also been two failed fostering
attempts and when the placement at the family group home broke
down, a longish spell in an assessment centre.

A combination of factors led to his referral for psychotherapy.
Some of the staff of the adolescent unit felt he contained an immense
explosiveness and violence. For instance, disciplining him sometimes
led to an escalating situation in which more and more physical
restraint would be felt to be needed as he became correspondingly
wilder and out of control. In these crises, as a kind of climax he
sometimes acted in an apparently suicidal way. What added weight to
the idea of referral was that others on the staff felt, on the contrary, that he evoked a tenderness and warmth in them and responded confidingly to them. A further weight was added by psychological testing which showed him to be highly intelligent and
imaginative.

He came to me for therapy, therefore, bringing with him a lot of
pressure that he should be helped. Yet, in coming, he showed very
little obvious sign of wanting to co-operate. He said little. Often
he was silent for the whole session. One of the things he did say,
quite early on, was that 'they'd' sent him here but he 'didn't want
to come.' Yet he did come, though often with an air of resistance.
Instead of talking to me, he would eat sweets and read comics, do
word puzzles, sort out collections of various kinds, do his homework
or just huddle down in his anorak, perhaps fiddling with a biro or
a zip or paper-clip. He would usually ignore my comments, answer
'Dunno' or merely shrug in response to my questions, and even
occasionally turn away and put his fingers in his ears. At times, he
seemed very hostile and I came to understand the fear that, if
pushed, he would explode. Faced with this you might respond in an

emotional way to the face value of the communication, with despair, for instance, or with anger. Yet you might also grasp that this silence is not just a wilful rejection. It is a defence against anxiety: he is silent and hiding behind war comics primarily because he is afraid.

So long as I was patient Leroy did go on coming, often bringing himself, and I was able to notice that this silence was not a uniform standard withdrawal, but would show all sorts of subtle variations, including softness, and that he would from time to time talk or show me things that gave occasional moments of access to his feelings, once or twice in a startlingly abrupt, direct way. Linking together the odd remarks he did make from time to time with his behaviour in the silent, apparently uncommunicative sessions, it also became possible to see that the withdrawal was not only just something that one had to endure while waiting for the real stuff of therapy to take place. In those sessions a state of mind was being forcefully communicated by being shown, acted out, and repeated, not just talked about, so that I could know through experience something of what it felt like to be on the receiving end.

When one looked in this way, what could be seen then was an attempt to avoid relating to people in a personal, emotional way, but to search out instead and hold on to the apparently more dependable, purely functional aspects of human relationships. Feelings, evoked by too much human contact, were felt to be dangerous, explosive, catastrophic, like a spilling of acids on hot metal.

Protection was sought by searching for order of a quasi-impersonal kind, for instance in rule-bound activities and situations. Leroy constantly used his intelligence to find and seize such order, to become an expert practitioner in it. The therapy became for him first and foremost a 'thing' that was predictable and the relationship to me as a person was secondary to this. In so far as I was valued, it was because I was felt to play a relatively minor part in allowing this to occur. When his occupation of the therapy 'thing' was felt to be secure, his relationship to it softened, and the room, the couch, the time, the silence were felt to be peaceful, receptive, gentle, lulling. When I was felt to be interfering, intruding, poking into him with my demands, the state of order became a fortress for him to hide inside, implacable, unreachable, slamming me, the enemy, out.

A second form of the attempt to substitute thing for person was in his preoccupation with material goods, things that could be got, possessed, devoured, had. What could be gained just from being with someone, he seemed to suggest, was a despicable nothing compared with booty that could be seized. And so he brought things of his own with him, session after session, and enjoyed them with some triumph.

In so far as he enjoyed coming, it was, so to speak, the room and not me he was coming to. What I provided - thinking, listening, a space, etc. - was contemptible, empty air, a bag of nothing: sweets, comics, collections of things were what counted. He would be in a fortress: I was the enemy. He was the one who shut me out, gave me a bag of fresh air for my trouble. I thought thinking about things was important, did I? Well, it was hardly worth having, but he would have that too. And so he would bring crosswords, word games, jumbled collections and puzzle them out.

On the receiving end of this, what was hard to hold on to adequately at the time, behind this defensive turning of the tables, was the profundity of his belief in and longing for an ideal relationship to a predictable, reliable, always fair, receptive object who would supply all his material needs in abundance and who would provide at the same time a kind of balm for his feelings, removing the terror of persecuting invasion and of a scalding spilling of destructive emotions.

A further technical problem illustrated by Leroy is the difficulty of predicting response to therapy.

Leroy's psychological assessment had, in the first place, left the psychologist in a quandary. On one hand he commented on Leroy's remarkable intellectual abilities, active phantasy life, and keen powers of observation. He noted, 'I expect him to be a rewarding boy to teach and he may well use learning as a way to help him cope with troubled feelings.' On the other hand, however, it was difficult for the psychologist to make a close relationship during the assessment and the projective tests showed Leroy's tendency to retreat from disturbing aggressive feelings, in the event only too well borne out by Leroy's behaviour in therapy. But glimpses of his imaginative capacity were seen by the therapist, very occasionally, in the obvious content of what he said, and more often in a kind of play of irony behind the sparse communications, or even by the very sparseness itself.

Assessing a child's suitability for psychotherapy is a complicated process, involving matching the information available about the child, his abilities and needs, with the psychotherapy and the demands it makes. Often one cannot predict the outcome and must rely on a trial period to see how it goes.

Later reports that Leroy is doing well have confirmed not only the psychologist's expectations but have indicated that Leroy might have made more use of therapy than he allowed his therapist at the time to think.

In the next chapter, further aspects of psychological assessment of deprived children are discussed.

7 PSYCHOLOGICAL ASSESSMENT

Eva Holmes

Psychologists do not often assess children in care unless a court report is needed or a child is admitted to an assessment centre, often after a family crisis or a foster breakdown. The observations in this chapter, however, are based on the unusual experience of being the educational psychologist attached to several children's homes in a London borough. I was asked to see children in long-term residential care who presented chronic learning difficulties, and young children with serious behaviour difficulties for whom decisions about fostering or rehabilitation had to be made, as well as a number of older children whose problems appeared to increase at adolescence.

The low self-esteem of these children has been described already. What became evident was that teachers, care staff and social workers often shared these low expectations of the children and this seemed to account for their failure to refer them for any kind of special help. It was taken for granted that all children in care would have learning difficulties and poor school reports. The possibility of remedial help was rarely considered, sometimes because of a mistaken concern not to label a child still more, sometimes because of uncertainty about the future. Perhaps previous psychologists had stated the obvious: he is disturbed and underfunctioning because of his disturbed background. To avoid this trap I tried to ensure that my observations and the results of testing contributed in follow-up discussions with care staff to a more detailed understanding of how a child was feeling as well as why he might be failing. I also made every effort to ensure that the assessment resulted, where appropriate, in the implementation of remedial help, psychotherapy, special schooling or a reconsideration of long-term plans. At the very least, a meeting of teachers, care staff and social workers took place, often for the first time. In short, I saw the role of the educational psychologist as more interventionist than just offering advice in reports. In the case of the very young children I assessed, this led eventually to the setting up of a special education unit described more fully elsewhere (Holmes 1980).

What, then, is the purpose of a psychological assessment of a child in care? Often the referral was a cry for help, as if to say, 'We cannot cope at school, this child is too disruptive or backward.' Sometimes care staff want a field worker to take a decision about placement and use the referral as a prod, or a social worker has to make a very difficult decision and wants an outside view of the child's development. The psychologist is expected to make a placement recommendation: moving the child on to the imagined 'better care' elsewhere.

By far the most frequent referrals came when children were
either 5 or 11, that is, soon after an educational change. This drew
my attention to the special sensitivity of deprived children to
transitions that other children can manage more easily. I therefore
tried to encourage earlier referrals so that problems associated
with starting school or changes of school could be foreseen and
plans made to facilitate them. Most important of all, however, was
the use of an assessment as a means of focusing everyone's attention on a child and his everyday needs for educational support:
someone to hear him read, go to his school on his behalf, help him
with his homework, talk to him about his future, explain perhaps
again and again why he is not with his parents. Overworked and
undervalued care staff readily accept minimal involvement with the
education and leisure of the children in their care and the children
easily feel that no one is interested in their progress. Their motivation to succeed may then rapidly evaporate and school be seen as
another place where you can be forgotten and no one cares. This
form of chronic educational neglect can come to light when an
assessment is discussed and someone will then take a renewed and
personal interest in a child. Without such a commitment regular
therapy could not be maintained, as has been discussed in Chapters
1, 12 and 13.

An assessment then involves some measure of current intellectual
functioning. The IQ is likely to be lower than expected, but what is
important is the opportunity to see how a child tackles problems,
reacts to success and failure, his persistence, ability to admit
ignorance, his response to praise and encouragement. Specific gaps
in knowledge often associated with school changes become apparent.
Measures of reading, spelling and arithmetic lead naturally to a
discussion about school and a child's attitudes and expectations:
perhaps there is one teacher who is respected and liked. How
persecuted does the child feel, how hopeless or insignificant?
Projective tests, discussed more fully later, provide some indications
of how a child feels about himself and his family. The assessment
essentially concentrates attention on a child, adding a more objec-
tive dimension to other people's subjective observations.

The experiences and feelings which many of these children have
had to contend with have a serious impact on their capacity to think
and to learn. This seems to manifest itself in very different ways at
different ages. The pre-school and infant school children, the 7-
to 12-year-olds and the adolescents will be discussed separately,
although in practice there is of course considerable overlap.

Whenever possible I tested young children in a familiar setting,
the residential nursery or their school. The assessment always
included some observation of behaviour in their group. The total
lack of caution with which these young children accepted a total
stranger, even in an unfamiliar clinic setting, was so common it was
difficult to remember how atypical of young children such behaviour
is. These children were never so involved with or attached to what
they were doing, or to the adult they were with, that they resented
an interruption. It became clear that being alone in a room with an

adult who attended fully to them was a unique experience. It made some children very excitable so that it was often difficult to bring the interview to an end. For some it was not the adult but the toys which were of supreme interest and a desperate wish to keep the test toys could be quite difficult to manage.

There is no ideal test for young children, and psychologists will each have their own preference. However it is essential to use a test with which the tester is very familiar, as these children tend to be exceptionally restless. They grab the test material, tear cards, throw bricks and take control of the situation with considerable determination. In addition to their lack of concentration, their inability to listen is one of their most handicapping characteristics. It was often impossible to be sure if failure to answer was because a child did not know the answer or had not listened to the question. I found that I was forced to alter my style: I spoke at half my usual speed, even with older children, and made sure, by calling his or her name, that I had a child's attention before asking a question or giving an instruction. Careful observation of these difficulties in listening and attending were helpful to teachers and explained discrepancies such as comparatively well developed vocabularies of nouns, but a failure to understand the little words such as in, under, before, when, etc. In sentences with subordinate clauses many children would respond to a key noun and ignore the rest. Their lack of experience of any sustained conversation with adults explained to a large extent why they failed to do what the teacher asked.

A research project with a group of pre-school children in day or residential care showed that these particular difficulties which guarantee school failure can in fact be reduced if the children are offered a daily, intensive, reliable relationship with a nursery teacher on a one-to-one basis, for as little as half an hour a day. Once they have a consistent experience of an attentive adult who remembers about them, they begin to be able to attend and remember themselves. Their restlessness was reduced and their below average IQs went up significantly.

Personality tests with young children whose vocabularies are limited have not been very useful although the Bene-Anthony Test of Family Relations can give quite dramatic indications of how a child perceives his parents and siblings. With 4- and 5-year-olds the stories told in response to the animal pictures of the Children's Apperception Test (CAT) are brief, but the frequent references to crying, being naughty and death, and such comments as 'where is the Mummy?' or like Keith's 'there is no Mummy' distinguish the stories from those told by children living with their families. They suggest that very young children in care need repeated opportunities to talk, and play, about their situation however painful this may be.

When assessing young children predictions about their future learning are always made with caution; with deprived children their inevitable restlessness and limited verbal skills simply confirm objectively the consequences of their impoverished and confused early experiences. It is important to remember that their backwardness is often a second-order phenomenon. Educational decisions should not be made on the assumption that a young child is in fact maladjusted, hyperactive or ESN(M). Such a child's behaviour may alter dramatically if very individual, consistent and reliable nurturing care in a family is provided. Therapy may help a child accept and trust such care more readily, as the treatment of Rachel illustrates.

Once children reach the age of 7 or 8, although often considered immature, they express their problems more indirectly. They are often overlooked, in spite of their poor school achievements, unless their behaviour warrants a special school placement. When interviewed in school, they still show the demanding behaviour of younger children desperate to be noticed. One child said, as she left the classroom with me, 'Did you *choose* me?' It is very important therefore to be quite explicit about the limited nature of the contact so that false hopes are not encouraged.

On the Wechsler Intelligence Scale for Children a familiar pattern of scores emerges: average non-verbal IQs but lower verbal ability with particularly low scores on tests of general knowledge, vocabulary, arithmetic and often coding. This evidence of a failure to take in information, perhaps because their environment has been impoverished, may also be due to their poorly developed listening skills and inability, described so vividly by therapists, to concentrate, hold on to and make sense of the events and experiences in their lives. (Occasionally the test pattern is reversed and children of average verbal ability show unusual difficulties with Block Design, Object Assembly and Picture Arrangement sub-tests. They may have neat writing and copy shapes accurately; the problem is not perceptual or motor but seems to be one of integrating fragmented pieces into a whole. This was characteristic of Tom and may be associated with a very early absence of any sense of being held together. The puzzle of a face also seems to present undue difficulties.) When asked to say what is missing in a series of pictures the answer 'a person' is surprisingly frequent.

The Draw a Person test also produced a very characteristic omission of arms or hands even in drawings that were otherwise quite detailed. This seemed to me to be an expression of helplessness, of an inability to act, but has also been interpreted as characteristic of children who have very little experience of being held, like Lesley and Rachel.

With this older-age group of children the CAT proved to be a very valuable way of getting in touch quickly with their feelings and ideas of family life. J.M. Williams (1961) carried out one of the few well-documented studies of this test with children who had experienced foster breakdown. She classified the stories into five categories:

1   normal family life
2   descriptive only
3   action stories without family relations

4   unrealistic parental treatment
5   loneliness and rejection of the child

The latter two themes were rarely found in the stories of ordinary children although they are common in fairy stories. The CAT stories of the children I assessed certainly confirmed these findings. They evoked a sense of loneliness and desertion often accompanied by a need to be self-reliant; the absence of supportive parents was striking. Sometimes roles were reversed and children had to be responsible for their parents:

There were two bear cubs and their mother and father were dead. So they had to work by themselves and buy their own shopping and play their own games . . . and they weren't frightened. (Card 5)

A very lonely rabbit and he was very lazy; he always slept in and didn't work at all . . . he had no job. One night he slept so long he died in his sleep because he had no food and no money. (Card 9) (Valerie's (Chapter 6) younger brother, aged 8)

In addition to Francis-Williams's broad categories, I became aware of some recurring themes; the pictures, of course, were designed to provoke stories about feeding, rivalry, aggression, etc., but the way in which deprived children respond is quite dramatic and extreme. A preoccupation with food was very common: there were frequent references to the withholding of food as a punishment, poisonous food, stealing it or to greed or the absence of enough to eat. Rachel demonstrated a more simple deprivation:

they bought milk, bread, food, apples, oranges, bananas, grapes, peaches, potatoes, cabbage, cauliflower, gravy and fruit. (Card 4)

they had cooked potatoes, pie, bacon and egg and toast. That was a good supper and for seconds they had bananas and peaches. (Card 8)

More primitive themes of biting and swallowing and being eaten were associated with violent stories which often escalated alarmingly with no external controls or reparative endings such as in this one by Tom:

all these people watched the tiger sink and they bit him but the tiger was only pretending to be dead and an even viciouser tiger came and his big teeth were showing and the monkey let go and dropped the tiger and the tiger ate the monkey. . . . (Card 7)

Another common theme was that of falling or things breaking apart, especially the table of food in the first card. Keith when aged 10 used the phrase 'fall down' ten times in five stories. His final story was as follows:

the door forgot to be shut, curtains blowing. Baby rabbit is in
bed and part of his cot is missing. There's a draught in the house,
he's not very well, he'll die.

Children living with their parents nearly always provide the rabbit
with a parent who comes to look after it, reassure it, protect it.
In Keith's story there was no expressed wish for such a person. In
other records, especially Lesley's, there was a repeated, idealised
wish for a rescuing, strong father who would look after a vulnerable
mother and child. Occasionally a story will illustrate the child's
phantasy of why he is in care:

A long time ago there was a family who always used to make fun
of their little baby and could always make him sad. They would
always make him do the cleaning up and the washing up and
always put him to bed early and send him to school late . . . and
one day their auntie came to tea and she liked the little monkey
boy and she brang her husband he liked him too . . . and they
took the boy away and made the other monkey go to prison.
(Card 8)

These stories often contain references to running away, and
being lost and found.
These CAT stories present a child's world which is unsafe and
unpredictable: houses fall over, fires start, people are eaten by
wolves, die suddenly and without reason. They reflect very vividly
the children's experience of sudden and unexplained changes,
helplessness, the failure of adults to protect them as well as their
sense of responsibility for their ill or inadequate parents and their
inappropriate self-reliance. These themes are evident even in
children who present few overt difficulties.
It is unlikely that projective tests in this age group can contribute significantly to predictions about therapy except perhaps in
cases like Tom's where the extreme dissociated violence was an
indication of what was to come. What the stories can do, however,
is to remind social workers, care staff and teachers that a mildly
disruptive, underachieving child who appears relatively 'settled'
in a children's home is in fact still very preoccupied with himself,
his past and his future and has a disturbed view of the world of
adults and families. This is best illustrated by a longer extract
from a story told by an 11-year-old referred for poor reading. He
had been abandoned by his mother as an infant and had had two
breakdowns of foster-care before the age of 5. Since then he had
been in one group home with stable staffing:

Once there was a boy called Peter and he was sad 'cos his mother
died and his dad died. His mother and dad died and he was living
on his own for some time. Then after two days was up he was
hungry so he went to a shop and didn't have any money so he
stole some food from the shop and he never got caught and went
walking out slowly and went back to the camp and he ate the food

so fast it was gone. He went back to the shop . . . the man saw
him nicking something and the police came and said: 'are you the
one who's been looking after on your own 'cos your mum and dad
died?' and he said yes and he had to have some parents, some
foster-parents, that looked just like his mum and dad; he thought
they were and pretended they were and was very happy and lived
happily ever after. (CAT Card 3)

This story and another one of a mother looking endlessly for her
children took us all by surprise and forced us to look beyond the
reading problem and to reconsider long-term plans.

Usually by the age of 11 or 12 children who have been in care for
a long time have built up an effective defence of apathy and non-
communication. Many of them may find the one-to-one interview with
an emphasis on tests persecuting, intrusive or irrelevant; it
inevitably draws attention to their limited general knowledge and
low school attainments. It is particularly important therefore to
put the interview in a context: who asked for it, why, what possible
help might ensue and who will see them next? It is also important
to discuss the results as fully as possible, stressing strengths as
well as weaknesses, and relating the results to the changes of
school and care staff that have so commonly been part of their
experience. Some acknowledgment of feelings of resentment and
anger towards teachers, and towards the psychologist, helps.
These feelings are often provoked by a sense of being lost in a
large secondary school where no one person seems to be concerned
about them. Their low self-esteem and low attainments attract
negative comments at school and all the feelings of rage against
adults who have let them down can become focused on the secondary school teacher who then feels that a child is over-reacting to a
mild rebuke.

The Revised WISC test profile is much as it was for younger
children. Verbal scores may be even lower, especially general
knowledge, vocabulary and arithmetic. Higher scores are found on
tests of common-sense reasoning and on those needing good observational skills, perhaps because deprived children have had to
learn to be over-alert and observant in an attempt to watch and
control their unpredictable environment. Older children in care,
girls as well as boys, are almost invariably underfunctioning
educationally. Even if they can read adequately they are poor at
written work and arithmetic; they show little capacity to concentrate,
especially if left to work on their own. These characteristics are
the end product of years of educational neglect and indifference.
Remedial help at this stage, as at any age, will succeed only to the
extent that the relationship between teacher and child becomes
important and valued.

Projective tests with older children are often unproductive; the
less defended violence and deprivation of earlier years is replaced
by emptiness and denial. They convey a restricted emotional life
and little capacity to think about themselves. Their difficulties in
thinking, and making links, already evident in their response to the

intelligence tests, are also reflected in their apparent inability to link feelings to events, past, present or future. They seem to experience life as random and arbitrary. Decisions about therapy seem to depend more on the degree of anxiety in the adults and the willingness of a therapist to face the 'brick wall'.

Occasionally, however, very disturbed projective tests suggest a lack of contact with reality or bizarre thinking which may not have become apparent in everyday behaviour. By contrast, some very disruptive and difficult young people may present themselves in a one-to-one interview as essentially immature and needy rather than persecuted and inaccessible. With such evidence from the assessment it is the responsibility of the psychologist to contribute this perspective to a case conference, rather than to collude with false optimism or inhibiting despair, either of which can prevent realistic plans from being considered. Where therapy is arranged, it is essential that schools, children's homes and foster-parents are offered support; a psychologist who has had some first-hand contact with a child can convey his needs and understand the difficulties he presents to others and is also then in a position to contribute usefully to the maintenance of the therapy. Where therapy is not a possible option, the psychological assessment, together with that of other workers, especially when links between past and present are made explicit, can offer a realistic basis on which decisions about the future of a child in care can be made.

Psychological assessments are still sometimes considered persecuting and unnecessary. This chapter has attempted to dispel that view.

8 'I'M BAD, NO GOOD, CAN'T THINK'

The statement which provides a title for this chapter was made by a child in care. I am going to describe some work with him which I think illustrates the first steps in the long struggle to come to terms with pain and loss – a task which faces all the children referred to in this book. Central to this struggle seems to be the transformation of pain from something which has the character of an overwhelming physical attack into something which can be carried in the mind as experience.

Ian
Ian Haines was 9 years old and had been in the care of the local authority for five years when he began once-weekly psychotherapy. He was an attractive boy with a thatch of fair hair but his face had something tense, sharp and hard about it. The difficulties of his life so far seemed to have left their mark.

When Ian was eighteen months he and his mother had left his father to live with another man, a Mr Haynes (spelt with a 'y'). After a few years this new family, including a baby sister, Tracey, broke up and the children were taken into care. Ian has remained in the same children's home for most of the time and was not considered suitable for fostering or adoption whereas Tracey is now settled with a family.* Erratic visits from his parents, who are involved in drug addiction and petty crime, are a source of additional pain and confusion, and his contact with Tracey is occasional and not close.

Although at 4 years he was considered to be developing reasonably well, over the following years the children's home found him to be deteriorating to the point when he was referred for treatment because of theft, minor fire-setting, and bizarre behaviour. His school, on the other hand, complained chiefly of his need for individual attention in order to sustain any concentration at all. Although he was able to write clearly, this would degenerate into scribble after a few words.

Both kinds of difficulties became apparent in his sessions. Although the sort of behaviour described by the home was more florid evidence of disturbance, I shall focus on his difficulties in concentrating, thinking and producing written work, and his capacity to recognise, locate and think about his emotions. These eventually came to seem far more fundamental indications of Ian's state of mind than the contents of his thoughts during the brief periods in which he was able to formulate them.

In considering what it means to speak of a child having to 'come

*Current policy might well be different in similar cases (see chapters 10, 12 and 13).

to terms' with loss of this order the notion of a capacity to process external events into internal experience becomes central. One has on the one hand some of the external facts of Ian's life and on the other the need to understand what the experience of being abandoned has meant to him. The link between these two aspects of abandonment is Ian's capacity to make something of the external events, to think and feel about them. This in turn depends on the quality of his early relationships and crucially on the opportunity to identify with parents who are themselves able to feel and think. Thus the legacy of the abandoned child is usually not only the burden of being abandoned but of being left with extremely inadequate mental resources to cope with a degree of pain which would overwhelm the most favourably brought up child.

In his sessions Ian made very little direct reference to his family, nor did he make much use of the toys and drawing materials. However, he had a considerable capacity to convey his moods by his general behaviour in the room. On one rare occasion Ian made an effort to explain the relationships and whereabouts of the members of his family by means of the small dolls in his box but the attempt soon ended in confusion and the comment, 'It's hard to know – if you know what I mean.' But what it was like to have a family whom you couldn't get straight in your head was something he did know about and which he could communicate quite vividly by recreating some aspect of the experience rather than by describing it. Only on rare occasions was he able to achieve a perspective on his experience which could enable him to describe it, verbally or even through play.

The indirect evidence about Ian's state of mind which touched me most was the quality of his destructiveness in his sessions. It brought home to me the distinction between a child who at a particular moment is driven by the wish to destroy and a child who, as well as trying to discharge his feelings, is also trying to communicate his sense of his world having been destroyed. He seemed to be conveying that he contained within himself a destroyed mess instead of the memory of something strong and good which could help him to begin to think about the catastrophic nature of what has happened to him. There were periods when Ian did become more coherent, when his activity was more like conventional representational play. On these occasions he seemed preoccupied with a hypothesis about himself and his family which was saturated with cruelty and allusions to Frankenstein, killings, madness and illness. These scattered references corresponded to the picture of himself which the children's home described. It was also, relatively speaking, comprehensible. However, I was struck by the fact that for the greater part of the time he was as his school depicted him – restless, empty and lost, unable even to think about terrifying things. At these times he poured out a stream of muddled questions or abandoned himself to random purposeless activity. At other times he appeared crushed by the sense that the jumble was just debris, the remnants of the Ian he might have been, which could only be conveyed by destroying his toys, box and projects and allowing his drawing and writing to degenerate rapidly into scribble.

Trying to pay attention when he was lost in this wilderness, unable to play, only able to generate an atmosphere, was very difficult. I felt I learnt with him that there was some risk of being misled if one concentrated on the things he had already been able to feel and think about and present to me in an organised way. One might then tend to let him drift away when he was in the grip of states of mind which had not evolved to the level at which he could talk about them.

In discussing the following extracts from the early months of Ian's treatment I hope to convey something of his underlying mood and its vicissitudes.

Lost   On one occasion Ian began to bombard me, as always, with a rapid stream of questions the moment he got through the door of the waiting room. He seemed to be asking something about the disappearance of a particular comic from the waiting room - did I know where it was? did I know? did I?, on and on.

During the session he repeatedly complained of not being able to find things in his box, scrabbling inside it and asking me if I knew. He scribbled 'shit' on a piece of paper used in some previous session. Then he added 'look at the ...' and trailed off into illegibility and ignored my query about it. He made a reference to Tracey, an unusual occurrence, then remarked on other patients having better toys and asked in which room I saw them.

Ian then went to the sink, and complaining that there was something the matter with the tap, stuck something into it and squirted the room with water until I stopped him. He rummaged around in his box, produced a white felt pen top and tried to draw on the board with it, complaining that there was something the matter with the chalk. He looked blank when I pointed out that it wasn't chalk. He then got some chalk and drew a tree quite carefully; this gave way to scribble and finally to the tree being obliterated. He nonchalantly dropped the chalk on the floor and stood on it, collected the chalk dust and mixed it with water in a mug. He found two glass paint pots which still had paint in them, seemed pleased and took them to the sink. I could not see what happened next but when I said that it was time to stop Ian announced that he had dropped them down the drain (thus causing a blockage).

In this session Ian had seemed in a somewhat driven and distraught state, for reasons not altogether clear, and the questions seemed largely directed at discovering what sort of state I was in. It was as if he needed to discover by experience whether I could survive his barrage or whether I would merely disintegrate into confusion under the pressure of having to produce bitty answers while he rushed on to the next question. At one point when he asked about Tracey he appeared calmer, more focused and experiencing something more straightforwardly like jealousy but he quickly abandoned that theme.

'Shit' seemed to be his comment on the heap of rubble that had once been his box and his sense that everything which might have

been useful was messed up and lost in there somewhere. Although
he had brought this state of affairs about himself through wrecking
his toys and materials, the atmosphere seemed to be chiefly one of
reproach against me. Like the child in the nursery rhyme who
sings

> Nobody loves me,
> Everybody hates me,
> I'm going down the garden to eat worms,

so Ian seemed intent on shaking me out of any smug thoughts I
might have about being helpful, and having the uselessness of what
I was giving brought home instead.

When later in the session he gave up being someone who could
draw a tree and became someone who could only make a mess, this
demonstrated what happened to him when he felt he lost contact
with goodness in himself and in other people. He then felt dependent, externally on me and internally on his memories, on someone
who did not give him what he needed – perhaps even burdened him
with events which were not just painful but incomprehensible and
not digestible into experience.

He seemed to feel that this state of affairs needed to be put somewhere, registered by someone so that they could take responsibility
for helping him. By putting the paintpots down the drain he could
leave with me something of what was sticking in his guts in the
certainty that I would have to take notice of it and deal with it.

Sometimes there would be little but an endless drip, drip, of
apparently disjointed questions: What was the time? Why did he
come? Could he have a ruler? Like the niggling questions of a
toddler they seemed to arise less from a wish for answers than from
an overwhelming sense of smallness in the face of a vast and puzzl-
ing world, and a need to discharge the helplessness and irritation
into someone else.

Confused Another time Ian began by asking if it was the holidays
next week (which it was not). He said that he had lost the paper
with the dates on... had I decided when the holidays were? Where
was his sharpener? (In fact it had long since been destroyed.)
Could he have one? Had I decided if he could have glue?

In this short interchange about the holiday dates which had
already been given to him in writing, Ian revealed how he felt that
his state of mind and mine were interconnected. If he had lost the
dates then I must be uncertain as to whether I had given them to
him, or maybe not even have decided what they were. If he was
confused that meant that I too was confused, and therefore unable
to help him, perhaps even responsible for the confusion.

How far might this image of me reflect his experience of his
mother and of other important persons in his early years? In its
good aspects his image of his mother and what she had given him
had obviously helped his development in certain ways and he could
be a very appealing and likeable child. However when he was con-

fused or could do nothing but aimlessly destroy, he conveyed the
sense of a child whose mother is so preoccupied with difficulties
in living her own life that she cannot help him in beginning his,
and eventually abandons him to his own devices. These 'devices',
probably rather frail in the first place, were now burdened with
the need to cope with the experience of being indeed abandoned
and would subsequently be further taxed by the continuous,
unavoidable losses consequent on being a child in care. Ian's crying need was clearly for some assistance in coping with this task.
The assistance required seemed to be for someone to notice and
remember the bits and pieces of communication which poured from
him, which individually were virtually meaningless but which
gathered together over time began to look more like a sense of self
and the world which someone could come to live with.

A sense of memory In the following session some of these bits
seemed to be drifting closer together, there was something more of
a sense of memory as continuity, though it all still remained very
tenuous. He started with a drawing in chalk which quickly turned
into scribble. He then began to cut up some paper very rapidly
with scissors, but it was not clear whether the results were inten-
tional or not.

At some point he put a piece of paper into his mouth. Making a
little pink and white ball out of plasticine he stuck it on to the desk,
then cut it slowly and deliberately with the scissors. In response
to my remarking on this he said that he had had a wart cut out as
a baby without... (I supplied the word 'anaesthetic'). Yes. He
told me that he was going to have another cut out that afternoon.
He had been at his other children's home when the last one had
been cut out. It turned out that he had been 5 when it happened.
Then he became more offhand in response to questions and he dismissed the matter saying he wasn't 'bothered about this afternoon'.

By this time Ian had gone over to the window and scribbled something in the recess while he knelt up on the couch. He then tried
to make a den on the couch as he had done the previous week, and
lay down covering his head with a cushion. He had been muttering
something while scribbling at the window and still made odd remarks
while he lay on the couch, most of them inaudible. Then I heard
him say something about a 'y' and an 'i'.

He went over to the sink and pushed bits of paper towel up the
tap, drew the child's seat near and sat down leaning right over
the sink. I thought that he might have been playing with the drain.
He touched a piece of soap to his tongue.

Ian returned to the couch and lay down. This time he remarked
with surprise on the fact that the cushion had a zipper – and said
he could use the cover as a bag for school. He wanted to take the
foam out. I wouldn't let him. He put the cushion between his legs
and ran the zipper up and down several times.

At the beginning of the session Ian had seemed to be in a state
where he could only scribble and snip. The activities had the
familiar, somewhat hopeless, endless, slightly accusatory air about

them. When he put the paper into his mouth it made me think about
a baby left to his own devices without anything in the way of a
toy or a blanket or a dummy to sustain memories of his mother, at
a time when he is not yet able to cope alone and can only get into
a state, or root around for any chance object to chew.

The general, pervasive sense of being unable to cope then seemed
to come into focus and took on a more definite shape - as if he
ceased to be adrift and became aware of having an incomprehensible
burden on his mind of which he could only try to rid himself, like
the plasticine ball and the wart. The burden on this occasion
seemed connected with the 'i' in his surname which linked him with
his father. There seemed a very long road yet to travel before he
could know that what he had suffered had been a human experience,
however dreadful, at the hands of other human beings.

Later in the session he seemed to feel that the room might after
all be of some use in travelling this road - it might yield a safe den
and a school bag and some help with his burden. At this point he
seemed to get back in touch with some good aspects of his experience - some time with his mother when he had enjoyed the protection of her lap. However, that sense of having what he needed
appeared very fragile and by the end the play with the zip seemed
to indicate that it was lost again.

These extracts were taken from the first few months of Ian's
treatment. They illustrate the very beginning of a process whereby
Ian might hope to 'come to terms' with his life thus far and so be
able to make something of his future. At first he presented a picture of someone utterly possessed by a disaster which he could
only display to others - being quite unable to deal with it himself.
The last extract, after about nine months of treatment, seems to
show that when he has gained a sense of being adequately cared
for a process of locating and recognising his feelings can tentatively begin.

I think that everyone who comes to be involved in this sort of
work does so out of a belief in there being a capacity of the human
mind to cope with mental pain. But I think there is equally a danger
of coming to take this capacity too much for granted. I have concentrated on the early stages of Ian's treatment because I think it
sheds some light on the foundations of our human capacity to cope
with pain and loss.

Postcript As these small beginnings may be difficult to relate to
our more ordinary experiences it may be helpful to conclude by
giving some idea of what took place during the next two years of
Ian's psychotherapy. As his mind became a more solid vessel the
change in the character of his pain, visible in this last extract,
was carried forward. As if concentrated and rendered full of poignant meaning, it would now overwhelm him in occasional short-
lived moments of wretchedness, comprehension and regret. One
example was his description of his enthusiasm for a martial arts
club in terms of the amount of concentration and discipline that was
required. Ian said sadly and simply that he needed this - his

mother had never had any self-control. On another occasion he
felt that some of his difficulties were of his own making. When he
had first come into care he had been quite good at school but then
he had messed things up for himself so that he was sent to a special
school with numerous dispensations. Now he wished he could be
just an ordinary schoolboy with a school blazer and a proper school
that had rules and gave homework. From these moments of brief
but painful clarity he would subside into various desultory activities such as comic reading, pop singing or building dens out of
the furniture.

For Ian the struggle now was not so much to rescue meaning from
emotional devastation as to be able to endure what he was discovering about the meaning of his experience. The outcome seemed to
hinge on whether he could feel his mind contained enough love
and strength to help him in his development or whether it was only
the bearer of painful and often unwelcome insights.

Ian's capacity to picture a world where love and thinking combined was dramatically affected by his experience of adults in his
children's home. For a large part of his time in care he was greatly
sustained by two workers who stayed for several years and took
a special interest in him, in particular in seeking psychotherapy
for him. When they left he felt completely abandoned to a constantly
changing staff, a continual reminder of his original abandonment,
and of the fact that there was no one to whom he was special.
Although he never again became so attached to anyone, the occasion of each staff member leaving seemed to cynically call in question whether he hadn't been better off as the 'nutty' one of the
children's home. For months at a time Ian would turn his back on
his potential for development and seek refuge in various images
of himself as crazy and not responsible for his actions. Each epi-
sode would involve a long struggle back to a saner self who knew
only too bitterly what was happening to him.

9 DIFFICULTIES ABOUT THINKING AND LEARNING

Gianna Henry

Many children who have been in care for a substantial period of time, especially early in their lives, appear to suffer from learning difficulties, as discussed in Chapter 7.

This problem is recurrent enough to suggest that a link can be made between very early deprivation and its impact on the equipment that is necessary for a child to acquire and retain knowledge, but most of all, to think.

Thinking is not to be seen as the unfolding of an autonomous function, but as deeply related to a child's emotional development. In many chapters of this book we have heard about children who suffered from the lack of a consistent caretaker capable of holding their emotional needs and anxieties. In describing a child who defines himself by saying, 'I am bad, I am no good, I can't think,' his therapist suggests that Ian 'had been left with extremely inadequate mental resources to cope with a degree of pain which could overwhelm the most favourably brought up child.' How could Ian possibly manage such a task with his faulty equipment? If we reflect upon this statement we see the problem is twofold. Firstly, the equipment is faulty, and secondly, even good equipment would probably have been inadequate to deal with the degree of pain deprived children are often confronted with.

I would like to focus, firstly, on the reasons why the equipment appears often to be faulty and later on the issue of the intolerable input.

Wilfred Bion has developed in his writing some extremely helpful insight into 'The world that is revealed by the attempt to understand our understanding' and the formulation of ideas by which thinking thoughts is achieved (Bion, 1962, pp. vii and x). He suggests that a 'stepping stone' in the normal development of a child is having the experience of 'a container', a person able to receive into herself (I am using the feminine as this function is usually fulfilled by the mother or substitute mother) a chaotic input of feelings and sensations, mainly painful ones. As described in Chapter 1, these feelings need to be held and somehow made bearable for the infant through a process that initially takes place in 'the container'. For instance, the mother of a small baby might be confronted with a very distressed infant who is crying and maybe even refusing to be fed although hungry. He is totally overwhelmed by a cluster of distress which may be meaningless to him. If the mother is able to understand the reason for his discomfort, give it a meaning, and minister to the child's needs she will perform for him what Bion describes as 'alpha function' (1962, p. 2).

By this he means that she will use her own empathy or 'reverie' (a process that involves feelings and thoughts as deeply inter-woven with one another), in order to metabolise in herself what the child is not, as yet, able to metabolise. Through this process, which will take place again and again during a child's infancy, the chaotic cluster of painful feelings and sensations experienced by the baby as totally overwhelming can be responded to and made bearable. Bion describes this process as transforming unprocessed 'beta' elements, often experienced purely at a 'protomental bodily level' into meaningful and thinkable 'alpha' elements. He stresses that it is vital, in this process, for the mother to use her own mental equipment for giving a meaning to the meaningless. Very gradually the child takes inside himself this repeated experience of having a space in somebody's mind and of being understood. This enables him to develop his own capacity to think and event-ually to develop a space in his own mind.

It should not be taken for granted that such a space exists and is there from birth, ready to receive the mental equivalent of food. Although I am using frequent comparisons with the digestive system, in describing a child's mental development, I would like to stress that while we are all aware that a physically healthy child is born with a stomach and the equipment to digest food, there is not an equivalent asset in mental development. The space in the mind and the capacity to metabolise contents, once this space exists, both develop only gradually. They are not born with the child. Unfavourable conditions may well interfere with their devel-opment.

We are often confronted with patients, especially amongst the ones who have missed out on the early experience of 'containment' as described by Bion, who do not seem to have developed such equipment. This was the case with an adolescent girl (aged 13 when she started therapy) whom I treated intensively for four years. Mandy had been in a children's home for the first six years of her life. She had completely 'forgotten' those first six years.

At the beginning of treatment I felt that my words were somehow gliding away from her; I had the disconcerting feeling that she lacked a receptacle for her thoughts and feelings. She suffered from very severe learning difficulties and was still a very poor reader when she started treatment. She gave a very striking exam-ple of the features described in Chapter 3 as the 'in one ear and out the other' type of child. When, very gradually in her treat-ment, Mandy developed a rudimentary internal space and was able, during some sessions, to stay, at least fleetingly, with painful thoughts and feelings, this was often a very short-lived experi-ence. She appeared to recycle something that 'could be thought about' (alpha elements) back into bodily processes (the evacuation of beta elements). This defence drained her of any insight she had acquired. It could take the shape of vomiting, or diarrhoea; at times I saw a version of the same phenomenon in her particular way of crying. I perceived strongly in the sessions that her eyes were crying, in order to wash away the feelings, but it was as if she didn't perceive it. She let her tears flow, occasionally blowing her nose, and in fact she told me herself, on those occasions, that she didn't feel any pain. A memory which had emerged only in her second year of treatment was that she had wet her bed until the age of 10. A rather alarming symptom was that she suffered also at times from heavy vaginal haemorrhages and she spoke anxiously about them saying that she felt 'that the life blood was running out of her.'

The image of a haemorrhage, as opposed to vomiting and diarrhoea, seems to me to provide a good model of the depleting process that often occurs in deprived children and is at the root of their thinking and learning difficulties. If a child consistently uses this evacuatory model in order to rid himself or herself of painful thoughts and emotions, 'the life blood' (capacity to learn) could run away with the waste-product.

It is a very rare occurrence for deprived children to preserve a selective capacity to think, learn and retain notions, reserving the excretory process only for intolerable feelings or thoughts. If they were better able to do this, learning difficulties would not be so frequent among them. At the times when Mandy 'emptied and flattened herself' I had the feeling that she reverted from a short-lived three-dimensionality, from having an internal space, to two-dimensionality (Meltzer et al., 1975) as a defence against mental pain. This is, I think, a rather frequent occurrence especially while three-dimensionality or depth is only a recent and still precarious acquisition. At the beginning of treatment and also when she reverted to two-dimensional shallowness, Mandy could relate to me only through 'adhesive identification' (ibid.), i.e. precariously 'sticking' to me.

This modality was very vividly expressed when she told me, close to a holiday break, that she had got 'into a state' at school and 'couldn't understand why', when she had taken the cling wrap paper off her sandwiches and she had seen it shrivel to nothing. This communication of the catastrophic feeling of 'shrivelling to nothing' and totally losing substance, when separated from a source of sustenance, was something I had been attempting to interpret earlier, finding no resonance in Mandy. In this session, I could help her to try to give some meaning to her panic, as she was still 'in a state' and had seemed almost to plead with me to find some meaning for the utterly incomprehensible feeling. This was an extraordinary occurrence at the time, as it involved the attempt to grasp the devastating symbolic meaning of an apparently trivial event.

I think it might be useful to make a distinction between paper-thin, two-dimensional mental states and hollow mental states. In my clinical experience, hollow patients are more likely to have once possessed a containing space and then lost it or renounced it as a defence against psychic pain, rather than never having developed an internal space, like Eileen (Chapter 3) or Mandy. A very vivid image of hollowness was given by a little girl of 8 who had spent a long time in care and also suffered from learning difficulties. She made a plasticine baby, which had a hole passing through its body from its mouth to its 'wee-wee'. When this baby was 'fed' by her the water went straight through and out at the other end. She was occasionally quite capable of thinking as Mandy was, in the phase of treatment I have just described, but could not retain this capacity consistently. One could describe this inter-mediate stage as one when there is as yet only a fragile internal container whose 'floor' easily collapses (as with Katy in Chapter 3). Bion (1962, p. 35) refers to the abdication of a potential 'alpha' function as follows: 'Intolerance of frustration could be so pro-nounced that alpha function would be forestalled by an immediate evacuation of "beta elements".'

I was struck by the content of some recent research on cognitive development carried out in an Italian primary school. A group of 10-year-olds was asked, as part of a questionnaire, to write about 'what goes in' and 'what goes out' of their bodies. For the sake of brevity I will mention only two of the answers, but at least thirty of them could be pertinent to the point I am hoping to illus-trate.

(Boy, aged 10) What goes in: dreams, words, sensations, feel-ings, pain. What goes out: urine, faeces, bad stuff and then blood and memories. (Girl, aged 10) What goes in: food, drink, dust, oxygen, spermatozoa and memory. What goes out: faeces, urine, babies, blood, oxygen, mucous, memory and saliva.

These communications confirm the perception of input and output as embracing the abstract and the concrete in an undifferentiated cluster or, to put it differently, it conveys the experience of a very concrete perception of mental processes.

Having discussed the issue of faulty equipment for thinking, I would like now to return to the problem of the degree of pain. The overwhelming mental pain and catastrophic fears aroused by repeated changes of caretakers were very vividly conveyed by Simon, a child of 8 (when he started treatment). He had been through a nightmarish sequence of in and out of care and changes of care.

Near to the beginning of his treatment Simon asked his therapist, almost as if anticipating an abrupt ending, whether he would be coming forever. 'How long is forever? Why don't we fall off the earth? If we fell off the earth and fell and fell would we fall for-ever?' He said he thought his therapist would move and get another job like Mr X, who had just left the children's home, and added sadly, 'As soon as you get used to things they change.' Simon expressed with great vividness the cruelty that he felt was inflicted on him by losses. Holiday breaks in therapy were always dramatic. In a session close to a Christmas break he scribbled on a piece of paper 'a plant grows in the soil', and then 'RSPCA', which was quickly changed to 'RSPCB' (cruelty to babies). At the time when yet another change of children's home loomed as a threat on the horizon, he sang in a session, 'We are only making plans for Simon - Simon must be happy, be happy when he dies.' The message appears to be, 'You are at risk of life and death if you find roots

in the soil of a relationship. You know that you will suddenly be
uprooted and there is no RSPCB to protect you.' The bitterness
of Simon's song is blood-chilling and gives an opening to understanding another communication of this child. His awareness that
his therapist was really becoming a central person in his life made
him feel almost attacked by her, as if to make him vulnerable to
future unavoidable pain. On one occasion, as she was attempting
to make contact with him, he drowned her voice by singing, 'It's
cruel to be kind.' While we had seen that Simon had preserved
and was at times capable of using a capacity to think, he slipped
into mindlessness when the pain became unbearable (cf. Meltzer
et al., 1975). One of his symptoms was soiling and this considerably increased at times when he needed to evacuate massively his
thoughts and feelings. It might be needless to say that learning
difficulties featured amongst his symptoms.

Martin, referred to in Chapter 1, accused me, at a time when he
was beginning to feel acutely the pain of the separation, of strip-
ping off 'the seven layers of skin that covered the soft spot'. When
we were close to holiday breaks, especially during the second year
of treatment, he seemed to put across a plea for me not to ask him
to bear the painful feelings. He told me, for instance, 'why don't
you let me rot in peace; six feet underground is such a peaceful
place. The brain only stops working when you are dead.'

Martin had become extremely skilful in using a procedure which
helped him to 'execute', to quote his own words, any feelings of
warmth and tenderness or the meaning of any insight acquired.
Muddle was much preferable to pain. The contact between us was
often disrupted as Martin had an exceptional capacity to make non-
sense out of sense, often by repeating a sentence of mine but
changing the word, e.g. changing 'character' into 'carrots'. He
was thus attempting to break links in my mind, in his own mind
and most of all between our minds. The contact was lost. Martin's
brain stopped working. ('The brain only stops working when you
are dead' conveyed strongly the quality of emotional suicide this
process involved.) But there was no way his face was going to be
wet with tears. 'Your face is going to be wet with blood before
mine is wet with tears.' Martin's approach to ridding himself of
thoughts was much more violent than Mandy's sliding into mindlessness and two-dimensionality, but whether thoughts are 'executed'
or evacuated, the damage to mental functioning is massive. A
significant consequence that is present in both these instances is
that feelings of pining, of missing a valued object, in its absence,
are bypassed in so far as the memory of its existence is obliterated.
We saw how Mandy had been capable of obliterating six years of
her life through 'forgetting', and Martin asked me to help him
forget that I existed especially close to the holidays. References
to a forthcoming break, but even more my very presence in the
room, were treated as unwelcome reminders of my not being dead,
buried, obliterated, or 'executed'. He was at times quite aware of
the murderous rage evoked by my disappearances, both between
sessions and during breaks. He told me, for instance, on one

occasion, 'If I am not in control, all you have got is the choice of death, hanging, electric chair, drowning or decapitation.' (Decapitation is perhaps the most significant of my options in the context of this chapter). Martin had used his skill in executing people when faced with separations on many occasions, as when his fostering had broken down.

This 'out of sight, out of mind', or perhaps 'murdered in mind' procedure can be a significant contributory factor to the impaired development of a capacity for thought.

Bion (1962) suggests that this capacity develops initially through an attempt to keep an object alive in the mind when it is absent. He actually stresses the importance of experiencing the absence as a spur to formulating the thoughts, i.e. to thinking about a mother who is not in fact there. This process can successfully take place if the frustration to be tolerated is congruous with the child's equipment at various levels of development. Children exposed to frequent and repeated losses may find it intolerable to keep alive the many 'absent objects' of their lives. They are attacked and obliterated.

Bion suggests that the space once occupied by the good present object does not remain vacant. The tenants of the empty space are now very attacking and persecutory because they have been fiercely attacked in phantasy. They are often perceived as internal monsters. This can help us understand the overwhelming anxieties of many deprived children. Their internal world is a graveyard milling with frightening ghosts. When alone, they are not really alone, but in the company of internal persecutors.

It appears to me that one of the reasons for reverting from three-dimensionality to two-dimensionality, which I have described earlier in this chapter, is perhaps due to the defensive collapsing of an internal space which is not only perceived as a receptacle for painful thoughts and feelings but also for nightmarish tenants that need to be evacuated.

This understandable defence can help us make an hypothesis about the impoverishment of phantasy as well as thought of deprived children. They may be using a self-defeating mechanism that faces them with a 'double deprivation' (Henry, 1974). In addition to their external, often massive deprivation, they are faced with the lack of imagination, vitality, and capacity to think and to learn. An internal space is a luxury which they might for a long time be unable to afford.

Many instances in this book describe the very arduous process in treatment which is involved in attempting the restoration of the patient's internal world, in facilitating the internalisation of a benevolent object which could give support from within in facing terror, anxiety and bearing psychic pain. I have tried to outline in this chapter some of the massive obstacles one meets in the course of attempting to facilitate such internalisation in deprived children. This is one of the reasons why their psychotherapy often involves a very long-term process.

The enhancement of their capacity to think and therefore to

learn is ultimately related to what Melanie Klein described as the basic source of inner strength: the internalisation of a 'good object... which loves and protects the self and is loved and protected by the self' (Klein, 1957, p. 188).

10 THE TRANSITION FROM AN INSTITUTION TO A FAMILY

Rolene Szur

Most of the children who have been described were living in small children's homes when they began attending for psychotherapy and most of them showed considerable improvements in behaviour which could be linked to the sometimes stormy course of the work with them. In some instances therapy seemed to have helped in preventing a threatened breakdown of fostering, as was the case with Katy. In a number of others improvement occurring during the course of psychotherapy proved to be a crucial factor in enabling the child either to move into foster-care, or, as in the case of Tom, to return to his own family.

Increasingly at the present time there is a trend away from children's homes and institutional care, and towards looking for fostering placements or, more hopefully, for adoption. The skills of social workers and others in finding suitable families to match the needs of individual children will play an essential part in this process. Even with the best arrangements, however, the family and the child may need help in adapting to one another and in establishing bonds of feeling and understanding which can provide a basis for healthy growth on both sides (see Chapters 13 and 14).

These developments are deeply influenced also by the conscious and unconscious hopes, fears and phantasies on both sides. Some of the children who have experienced the hazards of neglect, deprivation and institutional caretaking show very severe disturbance, and require more specific psychotherapeutic help in order to be able to adapt satisfactorily to family life.

RECOVERING FROM FAILURE IN FOSTERING

There are some cases in which even a brief period of time in psychotherapy may seem important if there is to be any hope of successfully placing a child in a family. When the gulf between a child's hopeful expectations and realisations, or between phantasies and realities, is too wide, it may be very difficult for him to develop clarity and judgment about his experiences, and a sense of his own reality as an individual.

William
These were some of the problems conveyed in a variety of ways by a very complex little 6-year-old, William. He had been taken into care at the age of six months, and with one or two interruptions had remained in care since that time. He rarely saw his mother,

who was a very disturbed person, and had no contact with his own
father. Hopes of finding a foster-home had received a severe setback when on a visit to a potential foster-family he had killed a
baby budgie, and he was then referred for psychotherapy assessment. With this history it was perhaps surprising to find a child
apparently intelligent, articulate and attractive in a freckle-faced,
boyish way.

In a comparatively brief period of assessment and psychotherapy
William showed in many ways his impulse to destroy anything which
could reflect or represent that vulnerable side of himself, which,
like the little pet, might trustingly seek to be loved and cared for.
Perhaps one might say that he felt that this side of his nature
had, as it were, been strangled at birth, and that he was desperately seeking for someone to go through the terrible experience
together with him, and yet maintain some hope of being able to
bring it to life again.

A mood of depersonalisation and despair appeared on one occasion
as he told a story of a mother ape in a film who stretched out her
arms and cried as she saw her baby being carried away in a river.
'And,' he added in a desperate tone, 'she didn't know that it
wasn't even a *real* baby, but only a dummy.' Implicit in this story
as he told it there seemed to be the image also of a mummy who
might not be real, and William agreed about this, adding, 'Pretend
mothers can be very cruel, can't they?' The eager, sensitive and
hopeful side of this child was constantly being subjected to fierce,
self-destructive onslaughts, destroying particularly those toys
and creative efforts which were the object of his loving care and
pride. Sometimes the sense of shock and distress involved seemed
to be mainly split off into the therapist. Then time and again his
longing for a good and trusting relationship would once more begin
to struggle back to life.

One is reminded of Freud's observation of the compulsion to
repeat in 'People in whose lives the same reactions are perpetually
being repeated uncorrected to their own detriment' (Freud, 1932,
p. 106), and which he linked with 'moral masochism' (1924, p. 165),
defining this as an unconscious or conscious sense of guilt which
drove people into situations where they would encounter distress
or punishment. There seemed to be an element of this nature with
William. At the same time there appeared to be a quality of un-
finished business remaining to be resolved, so that the situation
had to be repeated until eventually some new resolution could be
found. He always had a puzzled, enquiring air at such moments.
Perhaps there was some confused struggle to find relief from
haunting experiences by showing that he accepted responsibility
for his attacks on affection and hope, and by trying to bear his
own pain. It may be that he was also trying to find a way of
forgiving himself through understanding, and some acceptance of
himself as a more complete personality capable of loving and
reparative developments too. This theme, though worked through
to some degree in therapy, had still to be repeated yet again when
the possibility of fostering once more occurred. But on this

occasion fortunately it was in a somewhat modified form and, with exceptionally understanding and gifted foster-parents, has led to a happier outcome.

Some children may have such a need to feel totally accepted with all their faults that they are driven to making a display of whatever they feel is most unacceptable in themselves. Others may find that adoption or fostering arouses intense guilt, signalling final abandonment of idealised images of their parents, and they now feel identified themselves with the bad, deserting figures. Mathew, the child in the next chapter, illustrates some of this guilt.

Families receiving children like William often need to be able to endure many attacks on the love they offer, in order gradually to help a child to escape from the terrible cycle of moral masochism and consequent rejection.

GUILT AND SELF-PUNISHMENT

A very different child, an anxious and depressed adolescent girl was also caught up in a similar cycle. But, as her therapist explains, in her case the focus of the repetition was on a pervading sense of guilt, and on self-punishment.

Pamela
Pamela felt herself to be a very bad person, responsible for everything that had gone wrong. That meant her mother's breakdown and desertion when Pamela was 5, her grandmother's inability to foster her and her three siblings, and their consequent placement in a children's home. When she was 8 Pamela and the others were taken into a foster-family, where they had been staying together for some eight years. For this Pamela sometimes felt grateful to her foster-parents and regarded them as rescuers. But the feeling was spoilt since she also considered that the condition of fostering was a disgrace and a deserved punishment for the breakdown of maternal care. She thought that only foster-children had to help with washing up, and that this was as a punishment for having to be fostered. Although Pamela had strong feelings of affection towards her foster-parents, she also feared them. In addition she was tortured by a sense of responsibility for maintaining their well-being, sustaining their marriage, and the fostering situation.

Constantly Pamela felt that her best efforts turned to disaster and that although there was a good, mature and well-intentioned part of her, this was invariably defeated by a baby part which was stupid, forgetful, jealous and hostile. A typical incident illustrates this. Pamela tried to help with the laundry, but the washing machine overflowed and stained the ceiling below. Forever after Pamela felt reproached by this stain. She punished herself for a while by insisting on eating alone, sitting on the stairs so that her foster-mother felt her to be sulking and rejecting.

The central theme of Pamela's therapy was concerned with the phantasy of an extremely persecutory mother acting as a very harsh conscience within her. She was identified with this cruel figure, fault-finding, scolding and attacking every baby-like or imperfect aspect of herself. (One felt that if she should ever enact this internal relationship with a baby of her own, she could become an abusing mother.)

It seemed that it was this relentless figure that drove her in the repetitive cycle of punitive rejection. On one occasion she came to a session very pleased to be wearing a new coat given to her by her foster-mother, but within moments she realised that she had forgotten her gym shoes which would be needed for school that afternoon. This filled her with dismay and she spent the whole session tormenting herself, feeling unable to return to fetch them since this would be hurtful to her therapist and also her foster-mother would be angry at her forgetfulness. Yet in anticipating the return to school she pictured a horrific scene, of a furious, scolding teacher, forcing her to stand apart watching all the others enjoying themselves and looking down on her. Expecting once again to feel excluded from the happy family group, feeling foolish and unworthy of acceptance, she burst into floods of tears. As the session continued she partially recovered, but then, as she left the room, forgot to take her coat. When called back to collect this, she very readily saw that this was yet another repetition, one even more likely to make her foster-mother feel that her gift was not appreciated, and to set the scene for another round of incrimination and rejection. (In the event the gym shoes were not needed that day.)

This is a very small example of the driving force which compels the child to reject and be rejected again and again. It does also illustrate, however, Pamela's developing readiness to understand and gain insight into her difficulties. She gradually became less dominated by self-criticism, and more able to enjoy school and home life with increased confidence.

PREPARING TO FIND A FOSTER-HOME

In the next example once-weekly treatment was embarked upon with the hope of facilitating and preparing for fostering. As her therapist gives a brief review below, a picture emerges of a sad, insecure little girl, clinging to her hopes and revealing a number of features of the 'adhesive identification' (Meltzer, 1975) mentioned earlier in relation to other girls referred for help (Chapter 3). It seemed an important aspect of the work with her that it allowed separateness and separation to be confronted, and enabled some of the consequent hostility to emerge and be held, instead of permitting the clinging qualities of Rachel's attachment to keep 'papering over the cracks'.

Rachel
Rachel, 7 years old, was a resident in a children's home where the staff were hoping they might find a suitable foster-home for her,

particularly as both her teacher and her housemother were due
to leave in the summer. However she was considered a dull, unattractive child with a permanently drippy nose, and not liked by
other children.

She was the fourth child in a large family which had moved from
Londonderry because of the violence there, but had then squatted
in London. Both parents had drinking problems, there was marital
violence and periodic desertion by mother. At some point the
family flat was burnt out. Although for a while relatives had
helped to look after some of the older children, they were all now
either in the children's home or living with other families. Little
detail was known of Rachel's early life other than that much of it
was spent in the care of nuns in a convent.

It was striking, however, that she remained very loyal to her
parents and, despite all that had happened to her, still maintained
an idea of a good mother and a united family existing for her somewhere. As treatment proceeded this seemed to be a hopeful indication for future fostering. It also emphasised her near-conscious
phantasy of the therapist as a new adoptive mother, and the degree
of pain engendered by the limitations imposed by the treatment
situation was an experience which I shared with her.

I found Rachel a not unattractive little girl, with quite an appealing, elfin-like face. She accompanied me unquestioningly to her
first session, very anxious to be good, sitting writing and asking
my help as if I were her teacher. When shown the box of toys
provided for her, Rachel looked eagerly inside and took out the
family dolls, counted them but did not assign any roles or names.
She did not reply to a question as to how many there were in her
family, but after a moment said, 'We live in a new home now, the
old one burned down. My brother did it. My grandfather is in the
hospital. We live at M... now because of that.' Rachel said this in
an unsensational, almost matter-of-fact way, and became preoccupied with getting the dolls back into the packet, seeming upset
because she thought she had lost one. She then struggled to
count the animals but did not arrange them in family groups or
appear to know the names of their young or the differences between
the males and the females. She seemed to be conveying an impression of herself as only one of many with no secure position or
identity within any family group and considerable anxiety about
loss.

When she returned to her second session Rachel could not remember the route to the room and was visibly astonished to find her
box as she had left it. (Over the months there were many complaints that her possessions in the home were mislaid, damaged
or appropriated by others.) She told me a story about some
children at the home planning to run away though she didn't know
where. Clearly she was excited by the idea and I felt this first
little hint of rebelling against the limitations of her circumstances,
not giving up the hope of finding something better somewhere,
was linked with her evident tenacious holding on to an inner image
of good and caring parental figures, despite all the disasters in

her external reality. Perhaps there was a phantasy of running
away to this good home, perhaps mine, if only she could find the
way. With a great struggle Rachel then produced her first picture,
a bright red house made with sticky paper.

As the weeks went by Rachel's compliance and anxiety began to
diminish and, mainly through the use of a soft bouncing ball, she
was able to explore – over, under and around the furniture. Sometimes she would completely rearrange the tables and chairs so as
to give herself space and shut me in a corner; she would then joy-
fully demonstrate her physical skills for me to admire (literally
having to put me in a cage lest I go away).

There was a holiday of one month during which her housemother
left, and when Rachel returned to school she began in a new class
too. This first day of the school term coincided with her first
therapy session after the holiday, and she showed very clearly
how lost and anxious she felt with the many changes and separations. She seemed lost in the room, and was anxious about who
would fetch her afterwards. She ate an orange ravenously. Then
she tried to stick a small piece of cardboard on to her folder of
drawings, and after accomplishing this in an almost frantic manner
put everything away and remained still, as if afraid of disturbing
anything. During the term, however, she settled quite well at
school and seemed to be making progress.

Rachel's ravenous eating of the orange followed by her apparently
desperate need to stick the bit of cardboard on to her folder during
a time of particular anxiety seemed poignant evidence of her fears
of abandonment to emptiness and starvation, emotionally and,
perhaps, at some primary level of experience, physically. The
nature of her means for survival which came into play at this
moment was graphically portrayed as she stuck the little object
on to the larger one, that is, on to the folder which held the
pictures together. She seemed to be representing in this way her
need just to stick to the parental figure in order to hold herself
together, and to keep away chaos and emptiness. This adhesive
way of relating is likely to constitute a very vulnerable personality.
The urge to cling may make it very difficult for a child to express
anything but a surface compliance, or to show hostility in any open
way, so leading instead to the development of such symptoms as
those for which Rachel was referred – inhibitions expressed via
learning difficulties, or irritating and annoying habits like her
inability to wipe her own drippy nose.

During the course of time Rachel's use of glue, sellotape and
water to stick things could be analysed at several different levels
of meaning. This revealed how the sticky techniques functioned
not only to express her sense of 'sticking' to the object of her
attachment, but also to control and possess, to mess up at times,
and to cover up or obscure dangerous and frightening feelings at
other times. Rachel would, for instance, put strips of sellotape
across the door of the room and over her box, conscious that this
was meant to keep other children from sharing the room and the
therapist, or she would 'polish' the table tops with gluey messes

mixed with paint. In this way she seemed to want to cling to the
room and to her therapist, while at the same time the visits of any
other children were meant to be spoiled by these tacky surfaces.
One day she drew a dragon. At first she said that it was not
dangerous but later told me that 'they poison you if you touch
their spikes' and that sometimes she had bad dreams about them.
Towards the end of the session she covered the picture with sellotape, and turned it over, continuing in later sessions to maintain
this cover-up by replacing any defective bits of sellotape.

During the latter part of treatment I was pregnant and this may
have stimulated the little girl's feelings of neediness, revealed in
incessant demands for more glue, which I considered should be
met. However the awareness of the 'inside baby' stimulated her
jealousy and suspicions as to whether she was getting the best of
provisions or only the unwanted leftovers, also provoking unconscious wishes to poison the inside baby. She frequently made
bottles of brown mixture and begged to be allowed to take them
home to the two youngest children there.

Eventually the time was drawing near when Rachel's period of
therapy would be ending. She had been able to move forward in a
number of important ways, notably in being able to be more in
touch with some conflicting feelings which had formerly been
obscured or covered up by her superficially compliant responses.
One might hope that this was a development which could provide
the basis for more realistically good and stable relationships for
the future, and indeed her story had a happy outcome, when after
a few months she was successfully placed with foster-parents.

BEGINNINGS IN FOSTERING

When fostering becomes available during the course of psychotherapy there may be a direct opportunity to study and facilitate
the processes of adaptation. The experience of a psychotherapist
working with 6-year-old Charles originally referred for learning
difficulties, was illuminating in this respect.

Charles
Charles had been attending for some six months when fostering
with the prospect of adoption became available, and following on
this the direction of his treatment gradually started to change
course. This second phase began in fact to develop rather along
the lines of an exploration of some of the needs, experiences and
interactions which may take place between a child being received
into foster-care or adoption, and his adoptive parents. A facilitating person - in this case the psychotherapist - seemed to be
needed here as someone who could fulfil a role which was in
certain relevant ways close to that of a midwife, and in others to
that of a grandmother.

Recent studies of bonding and attachment behaviour, in particular with regard to the relationships between mothers and newborn

infants, have drawn attention to certain interactions regarded as innate responses. There has been some emphasis on a 'sensitive period' in the case of bonding, and on a partially mechanistic 'programmed' viewpoint, in the descriptions of the development, sequence and patterning of attachment behaviour. While these approaches do draw our attention to some vital factors in the development of such relationships, one of the contributions of psychoanalytic understanding of human behaviour has been the investigation of ways in which early infantile experiences and needs are not simply outgrown, but remain as an element of the psyche, which can be drawn on at later stages of development, by a parent for instance, to provide a basis for understanding a baby. Similarly, an older child or adult, at times of special dependency such as illness and periods of crisis, may become aware of certain feelings of helplessness and insecurity, and become familiar with the infantile areas and needs within his or her own personality.

It was evident with Charles that there was a deep longing for the fulfilment of unsatisfied needs at infantile levels, for the experience of the kind of intimate care and concern for his person, and his states of feeling which most babies may anticipate, and receive, from ordinary, affectionate parents. Sometimes it appeared that these wishes, and perhaps phantasies, had their counterparts in physical sensations. An example of this was his delight in having talcum powder on his bottom after a bath. Once when his foster-mother teasingly said that he only loved her because she did this for him he had answered, 'No, Mummy, you're wrong, I love you because I wanted you.'

It seemed clear that at a deep level of feeling these exchanges answered a need in the foster-mother also, to be in touch with the baby within the boy, and care for the baby, before being entirely ready to receive and devote herself to the more contemporary aspects of the older child. At the same time she was uncertain as to the 'rightness' of her responses, and evidently found that by occasionally and spontaneously sharing her experiences with the therapist as someone who also knew the child in a personal way, she was able to enjoy a sense of support and shared interest.

If we conceptualise the earliest bonds within a natural family as a binding together of internal phantasies and external personalities, then we may see a very similar process taking place within an adoptive family, though often obscured by many surface factors. When the fit between the phantasies, expectations, and realisations of the parental figures and these children is good enough, it may serve to confirm the child's sense of belonging. He can learn to define the realities of his own personality and experiences in relation to a real world, with some sense of security. This could also be important in terms of making sense of, understanding, and being able to learn about external reality. It looked as if this kind of compatibility was present for Charles and his new parents.

Commenting on the development of institutional children in adoptive homes Barbara Tizard (1977) remarks that a great deal depends on the extent to which 'adoptive mothers accept and even enjoy dependent behaviour more appropriate in younger children'. The case of Charles and his foster-mother not only brings this comment alive, revealing how the relationship takes place between individual people, but also demonstrates its emotional roots, and indeed its functional relevance.

11 GROWING UP IN FOSTER CARE: ONE BOY'S STRUGGLES

One boy's struggles: *Mathew*

Mathew began treatment when he was $7\frac{1}{2}$. From the beginning, he demonstrated to me both the tenacity of his grip on idealised images of his parents and the effect this had on his emotional stability. In his first session, he told me that he had two mothers and two fathers. He never saw his real father. He went away when Mathew was 'this big', and he indicated his foetal size with his hands. When I asked whether he would like to see his mother, Mathew looked at me in surprise and explained, as if to an idiot, 'Well, I can't see through walls and through the sea.' He asked me if I'd like to go through the sea. He wouldn't. There are bad fishes in the sea. And he drew the bad fish's teeth. In fact, one tooth was so big it took up the entire page. Then he drew me at the side of the fish's tooth, and said if I got too close, I'd be eaten up and I'd be dead. 'But you wouldn't be that silly,' he reassured me. When I answered that maybe he was wondering whether I would be like a big bad fish who might kill him, he told me I couldn't be because there is no water, and besides, I have hair and feet. And he told me the baby fish fight, and all their blood and bones come out. It seemed Mathew had to protect his mother and himself from any responsibility for the distance between them by attributing all the violence and destructiveness to some imagined monster. And we can also see how this projection left Mathew in a very confused and vulnerable state, as he inhabited a very concrete world but one in which he seemed not to differentiate between inside phantasy and outside perceptions, thus living in quite a frightening dream world. He tried to reassure himself with tiny bits of reality, but it all had rather a hollow ring to it.

Mathew's efforts to protect his mother took many forms. He told himself he couldn't live with her because she didn't have enough money. He'd like to be a prince with a horse with silver hair and tail, and all the rest in gold. Then he'd be very rich and could give money to his mother and then he could live with her. Or he would describe his mother as a much-loved but helpless princess who's been dropped at the top of a mountain by a fire-breathing dragon, and again, a little boy would have to rescue the princess from the dragons and sharks in the sea. And a third way of protecting his mother was to blame his foster-family for his and his mother's predicament. An example of this occurred the day after treatment stopped for the first summer holiday, when Mathew had a severe asthma attack. When his foster-parents asked him if anything was upsetting him, Mathew said he wanted to see his mother

(who lived in Denmark). He told them he had asthma because 'you
all do not like my mother and don't want me to see her.' Arrangements were then made for Mathew to see his mother during that
holiday.

One might ask why Mathew felt such a strong need to maintain
his internal picture of an idealised mother and to fantasise about
being reunited with this idealised princess mother in Denmark.
There are obviously many factors contributing to this need. One
factor, from Mathew's point of view, was clear. He made a flower
and told me it grows from its legs in the ground. If you move it,
it dies. I said that perhaps Mathew felt a bit of him had died when
he left his mother. He said, 'flowers grow, trees grow, peoples
grow.' But he later acknowledged that 'some people stop growing
when they are 3 or 4, and they don't look right.' (He was 4 when
taken into care.) A second factor in Mathew's efforts to maintain
his picture of an idealised mother was that it served as a very thin
line of defence against all manner of primitive anxieties. Horror
stories of cosmic proportions have always abounded in Mathew's
play and stories, as he enacts dramas in which there are suffocat-
ing quicksands, Dracula or cats turning into tigers. A third factor
involved in Mathew's idealisation of his mother is, no doubt, that
it protects him against genuine dependency on his foster-parents
and on me in the therapeutic relationship, with all the fears that
might imply. For Mathew is the only child of a mother without a
husband, and the phantasy of being reunited into that family has
served as some protection against all the normal rivalries with
brothers and sisters or with foster-father in his foster-family. At
the same time these rivalries are of course greatly exacerbated by
the fact that his siblings are actually the children of his foster-
parents while he is not. He told me once that he hears other
children say, 'I'm going to do this with my mummy, or I'm going
to do that with my daddy.' 'I can never say that,' Mathew told me.
And, of course, this is made even worse from Mathew's point of
view by the fact that he so obviously has one black parent and
thus can't even pretend to the other children in school that his
blonde foster-parents are his real parents. When the agony of all
of that gets too unbearable Mathew tries desperately to escape into
phantasies of an idyllic relationship as his mother's only child.
In a similar way, I think Mathew frequently tries to escape from
the full paranoia, terror and need he feels in facing the stresses
of his relationship as a child to me as a parental figure by trying
to focus both of us on his relationship with his mother in Denmark.
That this defence is not terribly successful is witnessed by the
number of times Mathew has become physically ill just before and
during holidays from treatment.

Much work was done with Mathew in the first two terms of his
treatment which helped him focus on his anxieties in the therapeutic relationship and begin to build in his thoughts an image of a
non-magical, non-omnipotent parental figure. When the time came
for Mathew's next visit to his mother, it seemed that our work
together had helped him begin to face the truth about her, and

also about his own feelings. The visit was to be shortly before
Christmas, and he told me he'd started to make a Christmas present
to take to his mother. He was going to make a nice little house
for her with children and a carpet. But then he said, he had something else in his mind. He doesn't know really. She's not a good
cleaner. Her room is a mess. She doesn't look after his things.
Later that week he told me he'd like to be a magic cleaner who,
with a snap of his fingers, could clean everything so fast. He'd
clean his mother's house, and then he'd clean her boyfriend's
house. I said he didn't really think it was the house so much that
was in a mess, but his mother. He said, 'That's true,' and he told
me, 'My mother takes pills that make her bad. She can't sleep in
the day or the night. I would be so tired.'

At the same time Mathew began to face the possibility that he
might feel angry with his mother. He drew a mountain, but the top
came off because it was a volcano. I said I thought Mathew felt
worried that he would explode with bad feelings about his mother.
He said, 'The bad feelings would come out and take over the good
feelings. You can try to put the good feelings back, but it doesn't
work.' Later he showed me with his hands how big the bad feelings
are, and said they try to get into your body, and they chase after
you. Mathew then kicks them away, because if one gets in, they all
get in. And if one gets in, it stays for years and years. But he
would trick them. He'd like to be so tiny they couldn't get inside
him, or if he was as big as a giant, so a cloud could be the size
of his little toe, they would be so small he wouldn't notice them.
I talked with Mathew about his wish to go to his mother with only
good feelings for his mother and to find a mother with only good
feelings for him. When he goes with angry feelings from the time
away from his mother, he's afraid she'll have only angry feelings
toward him.

This work, however, did not diminish Mathew's desire to live
with his mother instead of his foster-family. In the session before
he left, he put his head down on his fists on the table and seemed
to be crying. But when he looked up, there were no tears. He
just said, 'I'd like to live with my mother for the rest of my life.'

The visit to his mother that December did not go well, and I
think it is a measure of the desperate intensity of Mathew's need
to hold on to his picture of an idealised mother that he couldn't
tell me about what happened until about five months after the
event. But from his foster-father, we heard that Mathew spent
seven and a half hours with his mother, in the company of a social
worker. At the end of that time, his mother refused to separate
and followed Mathew and his foster-father to the airport. They
missed their flight because of her clinging, and the foster-father
went off to arrange a different flight. When he returned, he found
Mathew spitting out hashish which his mother had given him.
Perhaps not too surprisingly, Mathew reacted to all this with something of a regression to the same fragmented, confused, and
overwhelmed state in which he began treatment.

At the beginning of the third term of Mathew's treatment, his

foster-father decided that for business reasons they would not
return to Denmark that summer as originally planned, but stay in
England for another four to five years. This decision had quite
an impact on Mathew, as it became clear that he'd been living with
the phantasy that he would return to his mother that summer.
His efforts to deal with the fact that he couldn't live with her
continued to feature as an important theme in his treatment. At one
point he acknowledged that his mother had sometimes given him
bad things, but insisted that she didn't know they were bad, didn't
know what she was doing. Then he told me his foster-parents
didn't believe this. They thought his mother made him bad, but it
wasn't true. Then he wondered why I couldn't see his foster-
parents. I could tell them that his mother didn't give him bad things
because they didn't believe him. I said I thought he felt his own
anger with his mother was put into his foster-parents so he thought
they didn't like his mother. 'They do like her,' he said, 'but they
think she gave me bad things, and it's not true.' Later he told me
he was angry with his foster-parents but he never told them. He
was angry 'because they take me away from my mother. I want to
be with my mummy.' Then he said, 'I don't go in this family. I
knew before I came to Tavistock that I don't go in this family. I
want to be with my mummy so I can look after her.' I said sometimes
Mathew felt he would be the grown-up and look after his mother
as a little girl, as if all his own baby feelings and little boy feelings
were put into his mother, but then who would look after the parts
of him that still need parents. 'Say that again,' he said, and I went
over it again slowly. But he repeated, 'My mother will look after
me. My foster-parents think she's a little girl and can't look after
me, but she's not.' Then he said, 'I can never see my mummy. I
like my foster-parents very much, but I want to live with my
mummy.'
During the summer term Mathew was finally able to tell me himself
what had actually happened at the airport. This coincided with an
increased ability to acknowledge that it wasn't just the drugs that
made it impossible for him to live with his mother. 'There are other
things wrong. Her house is dirty. Her teeth are grey and horrid.
She wears dirty clothes that she finds in the street.' Once when
Mathew was little, his mother had found some clothes and tried
to put them on Mathew. They were wet. Mathew wouldn't wear
them. But Mathew continued to protect his mother from responsibility for her situation. He insisted that someone gave his mother
the bad pills. 'She didn't know they were bad,' he said. 'And
once you start, you can't stop.' He thinks it was a man who gave
her the bad pills. He would kill him if he saw him. He would hit
him with his stick.
Mathew saw his mother again at the end of May, and he returned
in a very muddled and confused state. The children in his class
were doing a play on the Greek myth of Persephone, Goddess of
Spring, and Mathew spent several weeks drawing pictures and
going over the story. His efforts to resuscitate an internal mother
from the underworld of bad feelings and depression were clear.

One day he was telling me again how the gardener betrayed
Persephone by telling the bad king that she had broken a rule
and eaten pomegranates. The gardener was turned into an owl for
his betrayal. I said I thought the owl had to do with the part of
Mathew that could see that his Persephone mother takes bad pills.
'She didn't look so bad this time,' he said. 'My mother looks so
young - we are like twins - we both like to draw and paint, and
we both have dimples when we smile. The one thing I don't understand is why can't I live with my mother?' I said he put into his
foster-parents and into me the part of himself that did know the
answer to that question. There followed a long, frozen silence,
and I lost contact with Mathew for the rest of that session.

I'd like to turn now to another thread which has woven through
Mathew's treatment because I think this has also had a great
impact on Mathew's stability and his capacity to relate to his foster
family. That is the theme of Mathew's relationship with his West
Indian father who disappeared before Mathew was born. He has
frequently been preoccupied with the colour his father must be
for Mathew to be the colour he is. Early on in treatment, Mathew
made it clear that his father was no more to blame than his mother
for his situation. He told me how he thinks he lost his father.
Once, before he was born, Mathew's mother left a note for his
father, saying where she was going in the country. Mathew's father
came home and didn't find the note. He waited and waited, and then
went looking for them. Mathew thinks he is still looking. Here
Mathew is describing his father as being as lost and desperate as
Mathew is. For Mathew has very sadly acknowledged on several
occasions that he would like to see his father, but he wouldn't
know him if he saw him in the street.

Of course, from early on in treatment, I was aware that the
violence and aggression located in the bad fish in the sea must
have something to do with Mathew's ideas about a different kind of
father from the forlorn and desperate one, wandering the face of
the earth looking for Mathew and his mother. And at times, Mathew
did speak about his mother's boyfriend as the bad daddy who might
have made his mother bad by giving her the bad pills, and who, in
fact, Mathew witnessed attacking his mother, bruising and scratch-
ing her face. But it was not until Mathew had been in treatment for
one and a half years that the full force of his fears about his image
of a bad daddy, as well as that of a neglectful mummy, came to the
fore.

At the end of his next visit to his mother she refused to let him
leave with his social worker, saying that he had 'come out of her
tummy, and was hers'. He ran out of the house, ran and ran,
pursued by his mother and social worker who fought over him
until the police arrived. At first Mathew was only able to tell me
about the incident in a flat, cut-off manner, as he seemed to be
still running away from the feelings it had evoked in him. But
shortly after the visit, Mathew went with his foster-family to see
the film 'Death on the Nile'. He had severe nightmares after that
and wouldn't sleep alone. He told me all about the bad couple

in the film and about the murders. When I spoke about his fear of
the bad parents who might murder him, he told me there had been
parents like that. He saw them at Madame Tussaud's, and at the
Tower of London. He always slept flat and frozen in his bed so
that if a murderer came in, he wouldn't know Mathew was there.
However these parental images remained severely split off from
his actual parents.

In February of the next year Mathew visited his mother again,
this time for her birthday. By this time the idealisation had very
much broken down, and there was no sign of Mathew's usual manic
optimism about going to see her. In fact, he seemed to be having
a very difficult time trying to conjure up any semblance of an
image of a good boy finding a good present for a good mother. He
seemed, rather, to have a dawning awareness that things might be
better for him in his foster-home, but this also made him feel
frightened and guilty. He told me a story he'd read about a rabbit
called Big Grey who lived in a lovely cage with all the food and
drink he could want. But in the cage he forgot about the meadow,
he forgot about the grass, he forgot how to hop. He had a chance
to escape to freedom, but he rejected it for the paradise in the
cage. What he didn't know was that he was being fattened up to
be killed. In the end, Big Grey was killed. Mathew here expressed
his great fear of what it would mean to disown the over-idealised
image of his natural, 'wild' mother, which had protected him from
seeing her other side. He would then be faced with his lingering
distrust of realistic qualities of kindness and concern and the
suspicion that his foster-parents, and I also, concealed other, more
exploitative motives.

After the next visit to Denmark he told me his mother hadn't said
much. She was very still. He didn't know why. He told me that
his own father went to jail. He supposes he did something wrong.
His mother went to jail once too, for one day.

The diminution of Mathew's idealisation of his parents had quite
a marked effect on his emotional development and his capacity to
relate to his foster-family and to me as his psychotherapist. His
teacher reported, somewhat sadly, that Mathew no longer drew
pictures of princesses, that he seemed much more like the other
boys in his class. His foster-family reported that he seemed more
settled with them, and in particular, was much more affectionate
towards his foster-father. And in his therapy, Mathew seemed much
readier to co-operate in the painful work of facing the intensity
of his infantile needs and rivalries in the transference. He could
no longer hide behind the delusion of being reunited with his
princess mother, as he now knew 'she always takes bad pills' as
he put it. The following Easter holiday had a great impact on
Mathew. Of course, he had reacted strongly to previous holiday
breaks but the reactions then seemed to be more somatic. He was
now much more aware of how frightened and angry separations
from me made him. We then continued over a period of years our
work together to help Mathew separate the extremes of his own
phantasies from the realistic qualities of his natural parents, and

gradually he was able to take in the images of the more helpful qualities of his foster-parents, as sustaining and protective figures in his personal inner world.

12 BREAKDOWN AND RECONSTITUTION OF THE FAMILY CIRCLE

Ronald Britton

In our society the family is the unit in which it is assumed the
child's development will take place. Our imaginative literature as
well as an enormous quantity of professional writing testifies to
the family being seen as the source of our satisfactions and dis-
satisfactions: the origins of our strength and security or the hot-
bed of our neuroses. The children written about in this book,
however, have suffered from a lack or loss of family life and I
would like to consider the position of such children and the
complications of trying to remedy their situation. I would like to
do this not comprehensively but from a particular angle, putting
aside consideration of the imperative needs of the child for physical
care, love, protection and attention, in order to consider the
family as the matrix for the child's development: the 'locus in quo'
of his personal saga. From this point of view the family, however
composed, provides a bounded space for the child which, when
broken, needs to be restored or replaced. The family seen from
this viewpoint is the receptacle into which the child is born. The
ability of the family, like a living cell, to maintain its own mem-
brane, its interface with the world, is crucial to its own survival
and the functioning of its components. When family breakdown has
occurred the child may or may not be homeless but he is psychically
unplaced.

Breakdown of the family as a psychic entity may in some house-
holds occur without formal disruption. This may lead to non-
communicating members fending for themselves in some less usual
cases. More often there is the incorporation of part-time members
(who may ostensibly be fulfilling a professional role) in its functional though not formal structure. Examples of such situations I
have met had a functional composition of mother, health visitor
and child; mother, social worker and children; father, residential
worker and child; mother, part-time father, day care worker and
children in lieu of mother-father-children, as well as several
variants of cohabitation and group life. I would like to distinguish
these from more consciously organised arrangements, whether
made by professional workers or inside extended families or with
close, sustained, neighbourly relations. What distinguishes these
latter examples is an awareness of the arrangements and the roles
and relationships remaining defined. In the former cases the
implicit, psychic identity of the arrangement is not recognised
and does not coincide with its explicit form. This leads to incom-
prehensibility for everyone and unpredictability for the children.
There are considerable risks that decisions of far-reaching

significance, such as change of worker or termination of crucial
arrangements, can be made unknowingly or lightly. This is not to
advocate an avoidance of long-term efforts to support and supple-
ment family care, but to point out the need for constant efforts
to keep clear the intention and the reality of the situation. A great
deal can be done to restore and sustain a 'family structure' by
combining imaginatively natural and professional elements (such as
combinations of foster-care with parents, children's homes, day
care centres, boarding schools and so on) where the original
family unit is not viable alone. As I reiterate below, it seems
necessary in such arrangements, however, that someone compre-
hends and articulates the whole arrangement whether this is a
parent, who must therefore be capable of it, or a professional such
as a social worker.

The children who are the principal concern in this book, however,
are not those in family situations where the breakdown is concealed or prevented but those who are displaced physically and
mentally. My contention is that such children need the restitution
of a framework for their lives that they can perceive as having a
continuous existence which will survive possible changes in its
component elements.

The psychotherapeutic process also needs a viable, comprehensible and predictable framework in which it can take place. When
the patient is an adult, economically independent and 'not too
disturbed', and the therapist is in private practice, this framework
can be provided by the two of them, though it would be an unwise
psychotherapist who did not consider the social context of his
patient at the outset. Anything short of this situation (whether it
is in the patient's psychopathology or degree of dependence or
in the therapist's institutional setting) necessarily involves other
people. In the case of children in psychotherapy the framework is
provided like an inner and outer circle by the clinical setting and
the family, though even in the most family-based cases school
involvement may play a part. Where family breakdown has occurred
the outer ring is formed by that coalition of agencies and individuals concerned with the total care of the child, and forming a
reconstituted family matrix.

In my view it is extremely important that the therapy is seen
by everyone concerned to be a process taking place within the
larger context of substitute family care and not as a repository for
parental functions itself. It is no more appropriate that the child
should use the psychotherapist as a parent than that he should use
the clinic as a home. In both instances he might imagine this and
he might want it to be so but he needs to see the difference between what he imagines and what is. The temptation to blur or
eliminate that distinction may be greater for the child without a
home or parents and for the adults responsible for his care than
for children with intact families, but it is not fundamentally different. Such is the nature of transference. The distinction between
the relationship to the therapist as a parental object and the
reality of the therapist's identity and role is always, without

exception, complex and hard to make for both patient and therapist. The reality of the distinction is the platform on which the fears and phantasies of the child can be played out in psychotherapy. The platform is supported by the clarity of the distinction in the mind of the therapist and all those involved in the total care of the child and the clinical provision for him.

Misunderstandings about this can lead to an abandonment of the necessary parental concern for the child by the agencies and individuals in whom this function is appropriately reposed. Usually this is the social worker in whose care the child is officially placed; the social worker may delegate a good deal of this in practice to foster parents, residential workers and so on but it has been my experience that unless the social worker continues to maintain a central function with intimate involvement, the overall, long-term consideration of the child gets lost. On the other hand a notion that the therapist is providing remedial parenting, or a taste of ideal parenthood, can lead to intense rivalries, often not consciously perceived as such, in professional workers and foster-parents. The need for clarity as to the intended functions of those involved in the care and treatment of children from broken families is all the greater because however well it is understood rationally it is inevitably invaded by irrationality and misunderstanding.

The reason for this can be found by considering ordinary functioning in family life. The limits of the family, however perceived, form the boundaries of an arena for intense loving relationships and the reiteration of personal and interpersonal conflicts. The individuals in the family not only interact openly in ways familiar to each other, and which some see as determined by 'family systems', but also play out their own internal dramas in phantasy and in action in their family relations. Thus a younger sibling may be the repository for a despised, rejected baby aspect of the self or a violent, tyrannical older sibling, a secret model of idealisation and vicarious satisfaction. The good and bad parents, for example, may become the permanent locations of virtue and give an extra quality of fixity to a tendency to polarise experience and rigidify ambivalence. Whatever the many variants of cast and possible plots, the breakdown of the family allows the spilling out of these dramas and provokes their re-enactment in a new context amongst the people trying to reconstitute a family circle. The breakdown of the 'circle' itself repeating the family disruption is the most fearful re-enactment, and menaces the attempts by fostering and adoption to provide the children with a new family.

Obviously fostering and adoption represent the most desirable efforts at the restitution of a family life. However, by seeking the most desirable solution too eagerly to acknowledge its difficulties and many failures, we risk the current wave of enthusiasm for fostering being followed by disillusion. Children will carry into their new homes their old problems and their old relationships which will sooner or later strive for repetition. I believe psychotherapy in conjunction with fostering may protect placements: however, it also exposes the situation to the complications of rivalries and

disruptions, particularly where these were prominent elements in
the original parental situation. It is common to find these struggles
taking place between social workers and foster-parents; schools
and foster-parents; schools and social services; clinics and any
of the agencies involved and also between different members of
the professional clinic team.

A realistic appraisal of the child's developing personality and
hence need for special help, whether this is psychotherapy,
special schooling or social casework, may run counter to the foster-
parents' wish to see the child and themselves in a particular way.
A desire to repair the damage suffered by some other person may
spring from the most creative aspects of our personalities. On the
other hand a determination to prove that we can, indeed, do it (or
rather to disprove that we cannot) may be prompted by a need to
rid ourselves of serious doubts about our qualities and capacities.
If this latter is the case it will be characterised by denial initially,
assertion later and possibly followed by strenuous efforts to eliminate
or control something felt to be potentially bad. Warning signs of
these incipient situations in foster-parenting may be a hypochondriacal concern for the children; an obsessive preoccupation with
potential delinquency; an increasing mistrust of the child and
intolerance of 'secrecy'; repeated efforts to eliminate what are
felt to be bad influences and reminders of the past. The ability of
foster-parents to co-operate with others in providing for such
children is probably as important a prognostic factor in the viability
of a foster-placement as any.

Such is the weight of difficulties carried by some of these children that a composite family reconstruction is necessary, for
example for enabling foster-parents to provide continuity whilst
not being the sole repository of parental function and expectation.
Combinations of boarding school and foster-home or the production
of a composite extended family may be possible if a sufficient degree
of co-operation can be found and if the whole is orchestrated by
someone (such as the child's long-term social worker) who sustains
an overall sense of responsibility for the child.

Many of the children referred to in this book are likely to
threaten the integrity of their psychotherapy and of their recon-
structed family circle with the disruption that their original family
suffered. In their treatment they stretch the setting and the
capacities of their therapists to the utmost. It is necessary therefore that the endeavours of the psychotherapist are understood
and identifed with by the people who form the human context. It
is they who also may have to put up with the 'acting out' of the
patients and become the recipients of disturbing feelings; it is also
they who may at times have to discharge a protective or paternal
function on behalf of the therapists. This includes of course not
only colleagues in professional disciplines but the management,
secretarial staff, porters and possibly cleaners. Occasionally more
dramatic eruptions transcend the clinic scene and involve such
alarming dramatis personae as firemen or policemen, or in one
case, as a result of convincing cries for help, an alarmed passer-by;

certainly the neighbours of the clinic may hear or see disturbing things.

The strength and viability of the context for the care or psychotherapy of disturbed children needs to be carefully considered at the outset and as far as possible the children protected from suffering the experience of their supporting framework once again breaking down under the strain of their own destructiveness or the anxieties they provoke in others. Unless the possibilities of disruption or disturbance are anticipated and provided for, or at least courses of action envisaged and realistic contingency plans contemplated, the potential emergence of new and threatening developments are not contained. For some personalities this sense of uncontainment provokes anxieties which lead to action and escalate the situation. For such a person, or aspect of a person, the sense of being 'uncontained' is linked to the phantasy that someone or something is refusing to take something in. At a primitive level this is experienced as a violent expulsion of awareness of the existence of the person, or some aspect of the person, and is linked in phantasy to being evacuated or aborted. In the psychotherapy of such a patient situations inevitably arise which correspond to this psychic configuration. At times the therapist is experienced by the patient as refusing to 'take something in' or denying knowledge of the patient's state of mind. At such times the therapist corresponds, in the patient's mind, to an object destroying the meaning and hence attacking the existence of the person of the patient. Frequently this leads to an escalation of violence of 'projection' towards the therapist and this can lead to action such as throwing things as well as hurling abuse. A scene such as this might be understood and disentangled in psychotherapy but it should be remembered that it also occurs outside the therapeutic situation and in relation to the total milieu of the child. Again a sense of not being taken in, held or contained can be experienced as a hostile exclusion or at a more primitive level as an annihilating attack on the reality of the child's experience of himself. This can lead to a desperate or violent assault on the setting, framework, organisation or institution involved which may well precipitate a further breakdown in the matrix of care. The determination to interrupt such cycles of disruption should inform the efforts of all of us in the field of child care and mental health. Our efforts to comprehend the situation may make it comprehensible and simultaneously receptive for the child. This requires a collective understanding by those involved.

13 THINKING TOGETHER ABOUT CHILDREN IN CARE

Joan Hutten

When children have two parents it is possible and usual for them to combine their separate perspectives when thinking about current management or future planning in a complementary way. 'Two heads are better than one' is folk wisdom that probably derives from a parental model. When children are in care or under supervision orders, the two heads can quickly become legion: lengthy hierarchies of field and residential social work, the courts, schools, clinics all have their caring perspectives, their specific experience of a child and their anxieties about which responsibilities they must be accountable for. To add to the confusion, liberal ideas about children's rights to participate in decisions about themselves can, in some cases, be applied without discrimination as a way of avoiding adult responsibility.

During the last ten years I have worked with a large number of caring networks over periods ranging from six months to seven years, to help in preparing and sustaining appropriate plans for treatment or placement (and a cliff-hanging process this has seemed at times). Referrals have come from a number of London boroughs and from the home counties. All of these have a very high percentage of qualified staff compared with the national average, and expect to provide a high standard and imaginative range of service and care.

In acting also as consultant to a voluntary agency's adoption project where skilled and experienced staff work with small caseloads of difficult-to-place children from all parts of the country, my experience of the problems in this field has been extended and deepened.

What can be learnt from this privilege of close involvement with developing children and their carers which may be of use to others?

AUTHORITY AND RESPONSIBILITY

Units of local government are known as local authorities and notionally people get the government they choose and deserve. The electorate votes for members of social services committees, who delegate to officers from the director downwards to the grass-roots workers in field and residential care. These latter, from their first-hand experience of individual children, may then seek permission to ask for specialist consultation. That is the way that we as a society deal with the responsibility we feel for others as fellow members of that society. Social workers may well wear more than

110

one hat in this chain of concern.

So far this seems rational and comprehensive – far more straight-forward than can in fact be sustained in close contact with the pain and conflicts of broken families, neglected children, and harassed workers. Greek mythology offers numerous stories about primitive sources of justice, altruism and responsibility, as prompted by a chain of blood-guilt and expiation. Although indeed innocent of murder ourselves, there must be few who have not at times felt destructive or murderous impulses. The need to make amends for such guilty sides of our natures or the self-righteous wish to punish such aspects of ourselves perceived in others may play some part in our respectable social endeavours even in an osten-sibly more rational era. We need to monitor the congruence between our efforts and the work that needs doing, if unconscious alter-native agendas are to be avoided.

Case conferences can provide a fruitful collaboration, but unfor-tunately they can sometimes become a forum where disagreements between agencies, or professional differences and mistrust may lead to a situation where decisions which have been taken are mysteriously sabotaged before they can be implemented. The temp-tation to seek the comfort of finding someone to blame or the reluc-tance to accept someone else's insights on 'your' client may uncon-sciously interfere with fruitful co-operation. It would be unwise to ignore the possible incidence of such ignoble, if all too human emotions, in oneself as in others, if one wishes to ensure that the client will not be adversely affected by their presence. It is only by recognising and acknowledging them that it becomes possible to resist their influence. Scandals in the child care field have aroused concern in all quarters. They have also aroused anxieties in social services departments which can sometimes lead to occupationally protective practices, more geared to maintaining control and avoid-ing blame or notoriety than to promoting the courage to make new moves in the hope of fostering real changes for the better. It is in this area that the intrinsic function of the professional worker is tested. In this context, it seems to me, the notion of authority needs to be linguistically differentiated from notions of hierarchies and bureaucratic practice. Authority derives essentially from the nature of the task. Action flows from our perception of the work that needs doing so that growth and development may take place. That perception is determined by experience, understanding and judgment.

CREATING A FACILITATING ENVIRONMENT

Very often it is the least experienced social workers who are exposed at first hand to the pain and despair of individuals experi-encing either crisis or chronic problems. What sort of facilitating environment is it possible for more experienced colleagues to pro-vide for them? How can we help them to relate the clients' reality to the resources available? My experience has been that if time

and space to think together about the front-line worker's experience is made available, the human resources can be increased out
of all proportion to limitations of material resources, however
generous these may be. It must be said, however, that this is not
always easy to arrange or to provide.

It may be useful at this point to disentangle the two strands in
service delivery that are usually thought of as inseparable but
which experience has shown can be usefully distinguished from
one another, i.e. the management of the case and the understanding of the complex interrelationships.

The importance of having one person who takes overall responsibility for long-term thinking and planning has been stressed in
the previous chapter. Nevertheless, sometimes the need for
administrative checking and managerial accountability can leave
little time for development of the worker's professional capacity
to think about the work. A variety of other points of view, even
conflicting perspectives, can heighten understanding of the interactions between family members and between family and team
members, and lead to creative development of the staff concerned.
It can sometimes be helpful if individual workers on a case can
have a private space to think about their client's communications
together with consultants or 'supervisors', who are not responsible for the management and overall strategy and co-ordination
in relation to the case.

There are times when it can be an advantage in consultation work
with other carers not to be carrying statutory responsibility. I am
then more free to draw on my experience in the child development
and mental health fields, sometimes less familiar to field workers,
who may not have participated in therapy and team work with
mental health professionals. Phantasies, misconceptions and stereo-
types on both sides may need to be explored so that the reality
skills and clay feet of both specialist and grass-roots workers may
be acknowledged and worked with. The notion of an 'expert' is
extremely counter-productive - two or more people, with different
skills and limitations, can only do what they can do.

Academic training courses expose social workers in training to
an ever-widening spectrum of alternative theories. Only in practice can these be tried out and used or rejected. Unhappily there
is a world of difference between academic broad-mindedness and
application. Only when theories have become digested, integrated,
and infused with value can they be imaginatively applied without
dogmatism in the service of clients. Sitting on the fence is as
unhelpful as ideological conflict with a client or with other workers.
It is possible to collaborate with social workers whose convictions
about behaviour modification, family therapy or psychodynamic
casework are at considerable variance with one's own by adopting
an heuristic stance through which both parties can discover a
way to work with particular clients which is responsive to their
needs rather than to professional differences. I hope to illustrate
this later in this chapter.

WHERE THERAPY CAN BE OFFERED

At the Tavistock Clinic we are fortunate in that the extent of our
therapeutic resources gives us the opportunity of thinking about
the experience of offering and supporting therapy, endeavouring
to learn from it, and sharing insights which may lead to new
applications both in clinical and non-clinical settings. In working
with parents so that they support their child's therapy through all
kinds of ups and downs and hopefully reach a fuller enjoyment of
and capacity to promote growth in their child, my experience has
made me confident that I can respect and trust my psychotherapist
colleagues to bear and think about expressions of both positive and
negative feelings without getting deflected from exploring and
trying to sort out their patients' experience.

I have learnt, however, that this experience is not what social
workers unfamiliar with therapy necessarily expect. They often
seem to conceive of therapy as some sort of mystique that it is
wisest either to idealise or to be suspicious of; that relations with
therapists must be about rival 'expert' points of view rather than
a complementary and helpful sharing of interest in helping a child.
I have also discovered that no amount of 'explanation' on my part
is convincing, but that a relatively short face-to-face experience
of the therapist and the kind of interaction it is possible to have
between members of a team reduces doubt and anxiety and engenders the possibility of ongoing collaboration. The detail of therapy
is private but overall goals and strategy need to be shared.

The kind of alliance it is helpful to build with parents is all
the more important in relation to the network which is concerned
with children in care. Unlike a one-off consultation which can be
taken or left, therapy implies a continuing commitment to think
together about the vicissitudes of the child's behaviour outside
therapy. It means mutual trust so that anecdotes about behaviour
can be thought about, that relevant intercurrent events can be
communicated. It requires effort and consistency to ensure that
a child gets to therapy on time even when he doesn't want to come.

It can be very difficult for the wide range of people involved to
keep together in a working team and requires constantly renewed
efforts as staff changes take their toll in the child's environment.
As a consultant to children's homes it can often happen that frequent staff changes lead to my becoming the main carrier of the
child's continuity, having been in contact longest and able to
link past and present in thinking about the child's cumulative
experience. This work, which is undertaken in the natural family
by real parents, demands exacting commitment from non-parental
carers if they are to provide the containment which enables children
to learn from and integrate experience.

The potential rewards from wide network collaboration can be
correspondingly widely felt. A group of residential social workers,
with whom I had contact over a number of years in connection with
'their' children's therapy, wrote a moving account of their lengthy
ambivalence but ultimate discovery that they were no longer doomed

to see children deteriorate in their care; that it was possible, with responsible stewardship, to return children to parents they had once felt competitive or hopeless about or to facilitate successful foster-placement. They felt proud and professional to be part of that process.

WHERE THERAPY IS NOT APPROPRIATE OR NOT AVAILABLE

Referrals for child guidance clinic assessment may be made at the point of reception into care or, more often, at the point of fostering breakdown or home closure where new plans need to be thought through. This may evoke perfectionist expectations that one has only to discover the 'right' placement to be able to implement it. In practice foster-home or children's home vacancies rarely correspond exactly to what is needed, but sometimes they turn out better than anyone dared hope.

Phillip had been in care since he was abandoned at a railway station in infancy. After three foster home breakdowns he went to live in a small group home when he was 4 years old. A change of policy about out-of-borough homes resulted in his being fostered by a couple who had been houseparents and were made redundant when the home closed when he was 9. He was chosen by this couple, whose experience of him had been that he was always well-behaved when one of them was on duty, although with other staff he could be much more difficult. Becoming a foster-child again did not work out as all had hoped. Phillip gradually reacted to undilutedly high expectations of good behaviour with stealing: first from his foster-parents and later in the community. This public failure was more than the foster-parents could bear and Phillip's social worker finally decided to place him with a temporary foster-mother within the borough and to ask for an assessment before making definitive plans. By this time he was just 11.

Phillip was monosyllabic and apparently incurious about what the various changes in his life might add up to but he did speak with spontaneous appreciation of the food provided by his temporary foster-mother. The psychologist who assessed him found him more interested in things than in people, not looking or hoping for help, and he feared that delinquency might continue and become a way of life if Phillip failed to be accepted in school or foster-home.

Phillip, his social worker, his temporary foster-mother, the psychologist and myself met together to take stock. We learnt that Phillip was attending the first year of a comprehensive school and was unused to finding his way about London like the other children but had been able to explain this to the foster-mother who had offered appropriate help.

From the clinic standpoint it was felt that Phillip was in no way ready to use therapy. From the foster-mother's angle, she was a single parent (of an adult son) who had grown used to taking a number of children for short stays. Her health was uncertain but she was a valued short-stay resource for the borough. The school saw no reason why Phillip shouldn't remain with them if he was placed in that locality. There were no alternative foster-parents available at this point in time. Little by little we sensed that Phillip appreciated this foster-mother and that evoked a willingness on her part to extend her commitment to him. The social services department resigned themselves to one of their short-stay resources being 'blocked' and it was (somewhat tentatively) planned that Phillip should remain where he was, at least until the next review meeting which was due in six months' time. The foster-mother said she would feel happier if I would attend the review meeting so that she could feel supported in taking on a more ambitious task than she had hitherto done. Since then I have attended six review meetings. The foster-mother has enlisted more than average commitment and interest from the school and in spite of sundry environmental hitches Phillip has achieved up to his capacity academically, has been involved in drama and other out-of-school pursuits and there have been no incidents of delinquency. His presence in review meetings has become increasingly confident and articulate. He describes the people in his present life with humour and directness and is a valued member of the household and their wider social network.

What made this satisfactory outcome happen? I suspect that the chain of realisation went something like this: fortuitously, Phillip's social worker had moved him from an unsatisfactory placement to somewhere that felt better - he liked this foster-mother's large helpings of food. The interested adults heard this and explored the feasibility of his staying there. The foster-mother felt affirmed by this bid from Phillip and by us for recognising it.

The borough provided a social worker from their fostering section for the foster-mother and Phillip's own social worker remained in post for a year and a half after placement and was able to make a planned and personal transfer to his successor. I undertook to be available for discussion any time that behavioural problems might arise and to attend six-monthly reviews. Phillip felt contained by this concerted effort and by the continuing liaison with his school, which had a system of year tutors who moved up through the school with their pupils, so he had as it were, for once, got in at the ground floor like everyone else.

Nothing succeeds like success! There may well be problems in later adolescence but at least there have been some stable years and a network ready to be responsive to change, which has enabled growth to take place. The 'containment' of the foster-mother enabled her to achieve and to provide containment for Phillip. What might be thought to be a generous investment of worker time has in fact proved extremely economic.

It seems to me that just as the residential workers needed to have the experience of living with children who improved before they could claim their professional self-respect, so field social workers and foster-parents need to have the experience that thinking with children and with each other about children can lead to individually tailored plans that actually work - they and their

children can grow together towards something rewarding and viable.
So much of social work is with desperate and chronic problems that
it is easy for social workers to become identified with failure and
patching up. Clueing in to the growing edge of children can become
a model for conceiving of the possibility of creative growth for
other clients too but social workers need to know at gut level that
it can happen before they can believe it enough to facilitate it.

The difficulty about therapy and its availability is that most of
us would gain from therapy - achieve further growth or the capacity to use hitherto latent potential. By far the majority of social
workers, however, work in parts of the country where therapy is
either scarce or unavailable and very many of the children they
are asked to plan for have had clinically horrendous backgrounds
in the sense that a skilled psychiatric assessor would be hard put
to it not to give a very guarded prognosis. Such a prognosis is
helpful if it alerts people to the dangers and difficulties involved,
it is not useful if it arouses helplessness and guilt. The assessing
psychiatrist covers himself by offering a pessimistic view of the
future. The social worker has to go on working with the child,
has to bear what does happen. If he or she does not take risks
by gambling on the possibility of a felicitous match between child
and placement no one else will and a demoralising cycle of deter-
ioration will set in.

How to manage this dilemma realistically, unsentimentally, but
hopefully is the challenge to professional social workers.

In the last few years important research and practice initiatives
have stimulated increased attention to the use of adoption rather
than fostering for older and handicapped children and insistence
on placing children with married couples has given way to some
very imaginative placing of children with single adoptive parents
who may themselves have had experiences which make their
investment in a particular child's future uniquely meaningful. It is
not surprising therefore that progressive authorities for both
idealistic and economic reasons have adopted a rule of thumb policy
to the effect that residential care is bad, foster-care is better but
adoption is best. Professional social workers have to take responsibility for deciding when it is timely to apply these guidelines to
individual children and when it is untimely. When fostering breaks
down, often for reasons of mismatch as much as inherent unsuit-
ability on either side, a child may well need a temporary haven
from the closeness of family life, and a period in a good children's
home can then give a later fostering placement a chance of success
that would have become improbable if a second foster-placement
followed immediately after a failure.

In the last few decades the task of residential social workers has
demanded ever-increasing professionalism in order to understand
and help children who, though rarely nowadays orphaned, have
frequently been exposed to major discontinuities of care and sometimes to the emotional turmoil of contact with mentally ill or addicted
parents. Residential staff, foster- and adoptive parents only care
for children on behalf of real parents whose positive qualities,

real or in phantasy, they must keep alive for the child while providing the reliability, affection and affirmation of the child's own
continuity that the real parents were unable to provide.

Unless field workers can think together with all the people involved about an appropriate strategy and timing for progressive care
of each individual child, society will fail to meet the challenge of
deprivation and with the best of intentions will perpetuate the
ideological injustices of earlier times.

14 FIELDWORK: FIRST VISIT TO A FOSTER FAMILY

Brian Truckle

One important aspect of the complex roles of the social worker when working with children is the quality of relationship which he is able to offer a child client. How to get to know and understand the child is often a worrying preoccupation, especially as major decisions have often to be made on his behalf. Hoxter (1977) suggests that with any psychotherapeutic contact with a child the first step is for the worker to have a 'space' in his mind for this particular person, freed from the worker's own preoccupations and prejudices, from the weighty luggage of worries about the last client or the next case conference.

Many professionals in contact with deprived or distressed children have frequent opportunities to offer a child this 'mental space' and the experience of being attended to, remembered and valued. At this point the child may feel safe enough to bring his own worries and concerns to the worker in both verbal and non-verbal ways.

Gary
An opportunity to do just this is illustrated by the following description of a visit arranged to introduce myself (then a social worker in an area team) to a foster-mother and two children. The previous social worker, Mrs Quest, who was moving, accompanied me on this first occasion to meet the family. Gary, one of the two fostered children, was home from boarding school. The other child, Lucy, who was out visiting a friend when I arrived, had made good progress with these foster-parents.

They were having much more difficulty with 8-year-old Gary, however. He demanded total affection from Mrs Clayton in competition with Lucy and he was reported to be 'taking over the household'. He began to have difficulties with sleeping, nightmares and sleepwalking. He was defiant when challenged and could close his mind to the foster-parents, particularly the mother. The Claytons were particularly alarmed by Gary's ability to treat them as things, by his lack of control of his temper, and by what seemed to be his compulsive lying. Nevertheless they wished to try to continue caring for him and to support their attempt a place was found for him at a special boarding school for maladjusted children. The interview to be described took place during Gary's first half-term holiday.

By his behaviour, Gary seemed to be testing out the Claytons and needing to elicit from them the rejection he perhaps felt he had experienced in his history of many changes of carers in the past. He was the child of two young, subnormal, unmarried parents; his

mother had herself been in care in a psychiatric hospital setting
from the age of 8, following her own parents' imprisonment for child
neglect. At his mother's request, Gary was received into care
voluntarily at birth, and at nine days old was placed with foster-
parents, 'with a view to adoption'. He remained there for nine
months at which time his mother suddenly appeared having acquired
a new boyfriend and a home, demanding his discharge. He stayed
with his mother and her friend for eight months with supervision
from the child care officer and health visitor. Standards of child
care within the home were noted to be low. The mother's homeless-
ness then led to a further placement for Gary with short-term
foster-parents. There were three more changes of placement by the
time he had reached the age of $3\frac{1}{2}$ years. There were indications
that he himself seemed almost to seek out these rejections. He was
negativistic, refusing to eat or respond to family affection, 'cutting
out of communication right in front of the family', or 'putting up
a wall between me and him', 'making me feel rejected and useless',
to quote some of the comments from the foster-parents. It was
decided then to transfer him to a residential nursery, where after
an initially quiet period, the negativism, sulking or temper tan-
trums reappeared, but gradually he began to 'settle' into the group
at the nursery and started eating better. When he reached the age
of nearly 5 he was considered to be 'fosterable' again, and placed
with the present family.

First contact with Gary and foster-family Mrs Clayton met us at
the door and introduced me to Gary who was standing by the
kitchen table, playing with plasticine on a board. Gary was a small,
frail-looking boy with a round, open, friendly face and a fringe
of dark hair. He solemnly shook hands with me, looking at me
directly, eye to eye. His look was amiable but appraising.
     There was a nervous dog on one chair. Mrs Clayton apologised
and said it belonged to next door. She was always taking in strays,
she said, speaking with a flood of words. She was so pleased to
see us, Gary had been such a great strain. It was a pity his half-
term was different from Lucy's. She had had to spend all day with
Gary, thinking up new ideas and activities. She was worn out.
Anyway it was nice for Gary to have someone special for him, who
would take an interest in the school. It was obviously a caring
school, but she had not felt that the headmaster had understood
her own point of view. Still, as long as Gary enjoyed it. She looked
fondly but despairingly at Gary, who had gone back to his plasticine board. He was bashing a hard lump of plasticine on to the
board, attempting to soften it. He listened to what was going on,
and from time to time darted glances at the adults. I sat at the
table so that I could see both Gary and Mrs Clayton, who was
busy making tea.
     Mrs Quest began to explain that I would be interested not just
in Gary, but in Lucy also, because she would be leaving. She had
apparently not been able to find an 'opportune moment' to mention
this before. Mrs Clayton said, 'Oh - well I did wonder. It's a pity

- I've just got to know you too. Never mind, it always happens
doesn't it? Well what do you think of that, Gary? Mr Truckle will
be coming to visit us instead of Mrs Quest. We've never had a man
visit us, have we? I think it will be good for Gary - you know [to
me] he doesn't get on with women. That's the trouble.' Before I
could answer, Mrs Quest began explaining the reasons for the
transfer, and engaged her in talk whilst Mrs Clayton poured out
the tea, and placed a large plate of chocolate biscuits on the table.

As this happened I looked at Gary. His look was still serious and
appraising. He began to roll out the plasticine, took some pastry
cutters and cut out shapes. Mrs Clayton handed round the tea and
said, 'Do have a chocolate biscuit.' I accepted one, and said I
wondered if Gary were allowed them. Gary gave me a friendly look
but did not take a biscuit. Mrs Clayton said, 'Oh, Gary has gone
off my food since he's come home from boarding school, haven't
you, Gary? It's not good enough. He always used to like his food.
We all do in this house.' I said it seemed that Gary was making
his own food now. Mrs Quest and Mrs Clayton laughed. Gary looked
at me directly and mumbled, 'Yes.' He quickly looked away from
me and then back again, with a friendly look. Mrs Clayton began to
talk at length and at speed about her difficulties in controlling and
interesting Gary, and how difficult she found his clinging to her
physically, since his return. How would she cope without Mrs
Quest? Mrs Quest answered her reassuringly, whilst I had one
ear/eye on them and one on Gary, who continued to increase his
supply of 'biscuits'. I felt that Mrs Clayton needed to talk to
Mrs Quest, whilst Gary through his eyes seemed to want to make
more contact with me. I suggested that I might get to know Gary
better whilst the two women talked. They both took up this sug-
gestion with relief. Mrs Clayton suggested that Gary and I go into
the front room. I asked Gary what he felt. He responded by showing me a balsa wood model of a table, taking my hand and leading
me next door.

I sat down on the settee, Gary on the floor at my side. I asked
about the table. He said he made it at school - school was 'all
right'. There were some big boys, but he had made friends with
them. All the boys had hot water bottles at night, but there was
no one to care specially for them. I said it sounded as though it
was OK at school, but that he missed Mum and Dad. Gary nodded
absent-mindedly. I tried to get him to talk about this more, but
he did not want to do so. He ignored my questions, and said, 'Look
at my table.' We looked together at it. It was painted brown, and
had cut-out pictures on top. I asked Gary to describe the scene.
He said that huntsmen were seeking a fox, but the wily old fox
was hiding and would never be found. We looked at each other
and shared amusement about this.

He put down the table and said would I like to see pictures of
him? Before I had answered he had fetched the album. He sat on
the settee next to me, close but with no physical contact. He
opened the album and we began to look at the pictures of foster-
parents and of Gary and Lucy. The pictures started with Gary

aged 8 and worked backwards. Gary pointed out who everyone was. A warm tone came into his voice as he said, 'This is Grandma' (mother of foster-father). I said she looked as if she were a nice person. Gary did not reply and went on to the next photo.

Gary came to one photo and paused, then looked up at me with a dazed look. 'This is me in this car,' he said, 'It is when I was with my other mother.' The warmth came back into his voice, but he looked very sad. He looked at me directly and said, 'I had another mother, but she died, you know,' and turned the page. I said that that was sad, and he went on looking at the photos. When he came to the end of the album, Gary hesitated as if he was reluctant to finish. I said I would like to see the photo of him in the car again, as it had seemed to be his most precious photo. Gary nodded and quickly found the place. We sat quietly looking at the photo for about two minutes, then Gary gently closed the album.

'Would you like to see my bedroom?' he asked. I said I would be pleased to see it. Again he took me by the hand and led me to his room. There was a bed and chest of drawers and a box full of toys. Gary went over to the chest and took down two ancient soft toys. Their original shape and colour was long ago lost. He introduced me by name to Bobo and Pedro, cuddling them to him. He explained that he slept with these toys in his bed, and proceeded to place them carefully under the covers. I asked if he took them to school. His reply in a surprised tone was, 'Oh no.' I said I expected they were too precious. 'Yes,' said Gary, 'they might get broken at school and anyway it's nice to come home to them in holidays.'

Suddenly Gary looked up at a picture on the wall over the chest. He looked shocked. 'It's in the wrong place,' he explained. The picture of a tiger should have been over his bed, and the one with a group of playing children over the chest. 'Mummy must have moved them while I was at school. Will you help me change them, please?' he asked. I agreed, at his request lifted him on to the chest, handed him the picture from over the bed, and he made the exchange. I lifted him down, and he stood looking at the picture of a tiger. I asked what the tiger was like. 'It is a *fierce* tiger,' he said with feeling. He smiled at me with his eyes and made 'attacking' movements with his hands.

Immediately Gary went over to his toys, looked up at me and said, 'I should like to build you a fort. Can I build you a fort? Have we got time?' I said we had if he was a quick builder, and he straight away began to piece together parts of a plastic fort, giving me a running commentary. The fort was to be quite a small one with platforms inside, and ladders so that men could walk about and see over the walls. He did not have enough ladders. How could he manage? Perhaps if he rearranged them. Ah yes, that was it.

The walls of the fort were looking a bit shaky, and the gates were open. I was about to comment on this when Gary looked directly at me for the first time in this fort-play and said firmly, 'It is not a safe fort.' Gary looked for soldiers to place inside. He examined them; many were headless or legless. 'I have broken them,' he said, looking at me sadly. I said, 'Lots of things to be mended.' Gary gave a slight start, and looked at me directly, his eyes bearing a deeply pained expression. He placed unbroken soldiers on the ramparts inside. 'The Germans are invading,' he announced. 'I don't think the fort will be strong enough.' He picked up a small green squirrel toy, saying, 'This is me,' glanced at the tiger picture, and proceeded to knock down all the soldiers inside the fort. 'I've killed them all,' he announced triumphantly, eyes shining. Then his face took on a serious look as he surveyed the battle scene. 'It looks as though you feel sad that everyone is killed,' I commented.

Gary turned to me with his serious look. Then his face gradually relaxed. 'No, not *everyone*,' he said. From a pile of broken soldiers he produced a knight on a horse in full working order; the knight rode into the fort, and by magic all the soldiers came alive. Suddenly, Gary was able to fix the walls, shut the gates, bring guards for the drawbridge, and install tanks inside to defend against the invasion. Inside, also, was the green squirrel toy, but it was apparently no longer to be worried about. 'Dangers,' said Gary, 'come from the outside now. The guards at the drawbridge might get killed, but the fort is safe.' Gary looked up at me, smiled shyly, and said, 'Can we show Mummy and Mrs Quest the fort?' He ran to the kitchen and fetched the two women who were still deep in conversation. They admired the fort and I explained the 'action' to them, and why the fort was well guarded. Gary looked intently at his foster-mother.

Mrs Clayton said she hoped Gary had not been telling lies. She never could make out when he was telling the truth or not. He had told his foster-father that he had taken the fort to school, but he had not – it was all lies. Gary's expression became blank. I said perhaps it was difficult to tell the difference sometimes between the real world and Gary's 'daydream' world. Mrs Clayton said maybe, but she just did not understand him. Perhaps I could help her there. She really wanted to understand, but it was so difficult.

We went back into the kitchen, preparing to leave. I said that it had been very helpful to meet Gary and for us to get to know one another a bit. I knew that Mrs Clayton and I had not had such an opportunity, and we fixed a date for me to call to meet Lucy, and then have a 'long discussion' with both foster-parents. Lucy would be 'quite another kettle of fish', said her foster-mother. 'She is a very withdrawn child. I *do* hope you will get on with her. *We* understand her ways, but to a stranger she can seem very rude.' I said I expected each person to be different, and would hope to get to know Lucy at her own pace, and in her own way.

Gary had returned to the plasticine. He was banging a hard lump violently with a toy hammer and then began to knife it. 'I wish I could understand Gary as well as Lucy,' said their foster-mother, sighing. If only Gary would not cling to her. He could go out to play in the evenings with friends from his previous school who called for him, but he would not go. 'Do they call?' asked Gary in a surprised voice, 'I didn't know.' Foster mother gave an 'Oh' of exasperation.

Mrs Quest said it was time to go. She would not be calling again, but might see the foster-mother occasionally at foster-parent meetings. I said I would call as arranged, and would also call at the boarding school and see Gary. I would write to him to let him know when I was coming. Gary gave me a friendly look and held out his hand to shake. They came out to the car with us. As we drove away, Gary ran alongside the car to the end of the road, waving.

Comments   I was expecting this to be a routine transfer interview, to meet the foster-mother and children, at which I hoped the continuation of the mourning for the previous social worker would take place. An opportunity arose, however, for me to make a direct contact with the foster-child himself. A first contact may provide a unique chance to 'tune in' to what a client is telling us about himself: his ways of coping, his defences, strengths and weaknesses, capacities and limitations; but the worker's struggle is to constantly be aware of his own assumptions and prejudices and to be open on a feeling and thinking level to communication from the client.

Gary seemed ready and willing to respond once he realised that I was interested and trying to communicate in his own language and at his own level (the making of his own plasticine biscuits). He then took the lead in sharing with me part of his inner world of conflict (Richards, 1971). It must be emphasised that for the most part it was Gary who did the leading and I merely followed. Where I attempted to initiate particular areas of discussion (e.g. about school or about repairing soldiers) he immediately showed the inappropriateness of those interventions. In fact, Gary warned me that those 'huntsmen who were seeking the fox would never find him.' The most 'active' part of my task was to communicate to Gary that I was able to provide 'attention', to create an 'internal mental space'. This involved holding certain questions in mind, questions like, 'How can I open up my mind to be receptive to this boy?' 'How can I free a space for him within my own mind and life, so that I can give him, so to speak, a room in my mind which is uncluttered by all my other preoccupations and thoughts and phantasies, including even my therapeutic drives, my will for him to improve?' (see Hoxter, 1977).

Gary responded to my interest rather than my pressure to answer questions, quite clearly indicating his willingness to use me as a person with whom to share his worries and conflicts including his concern and sadness about his 'other mother who died'; about what is precious and has to be protected (soft cuddly toys - representing his baby self - who are protected by his tiger over his bed); his willingness/capacity to see me as aiding the work of protecting what is precious; his awareness of his own emotional instability in the play with the 'fort' where he demonstrates the frailty of his defences and boundaries, and how easily invaded he is as a person both from without by the real world and also from within by impulses which he feels almost impossible to contain, except by magic. Not surprisingly, from his history, Gary's inner world is peopled by the dead and injured. What perhaps is surprising and hopeful is that he is still able to indicate this and in this way his need. The fort-play also seemed to demonstrate his fears of destroying yet another foster-home/fort, and his idealised hope of using the social worker/knight to strengthen it in order to contain him.

The tasks and roles of social workers working with children and their caretakers are multiple and complex. If we can learn how to relate and begin to understand the children who are in care with foster-parents or in residential establishments, this will have implications not only for use as a therapeutic tool in helping a distressed child who by the very nature of his status is likely to have suffered some emotional damage, but also for the development of the social worker's role as interpreter of the feeling and thinking of the child to the adult world around, be it residential staff, foster- or natural parents.

15 SOME FEELINGS AROUSED IN WORKING WITH SEVERELY DEPRIVED CHILDREN

Shirley Hoxter

The contributors to this book have brought to our attention a few of the children who get submerged in the anonymous, numbing jargon and statistics of the problems concerning children in care. The writers have drawn us closer to these children and have enabled us to follow each child struggling to communicate what 'emotional deprivation' has meant to him, or to her, as a unique individual.

The reader, like the therapist, and indeed like the child in the first instance, has been exposed to intense suffering. Now we can pause to reflect and to question. How can we bear to be aware of such pain? And, if we are able to maintain our sensitivity without being overwhelmed, how can we put this to use to help the children with whom we live and work?

The children discussed in this book showed that their lives were dominated by a continuing need to keep at bay the intolerable emotions of their past experiences of deprivation. Long-term work with the children revealed many of them to have a pervading pre-occupation with the complex of experiences relating to their sense of deprivation, which left little space in their lives for anything else, thus diminishing their capacity to benefit from ordinary maturational experiences.

Yet, despite the permeation of the effects of deprivation into every aspect of the child's development, almost invariably the children had little initial capacity to feel or think about their inner suffering. The therapist of Ian asks us to consider this dilapidated child in order 'to shed some light on the foundations of our human capacity to cope with pain and loss'. She writes that the notion of a capacity to process external events into internal experiences becomes central when considering what it means to speak of 'coming to terms' with severe loss. She considers that this capacity depends crucially on the opportunities to identify with parents who are themselves able to feel and think.

An expansion of these thoughts may help us as readers who are attempting 'to come to terms' with this book and also as people who wish to increase our ability to meet the children's needs. The crux of the child's deprivation may be perceived as the absence of an adult who, parent-like, shows constancy of care by being sufficiently present and emotionally available to be receptive to the child's feelings and to 'think' about them. The 'thinking' in this context does not require to be intellectually demanding, it entails rather the capacity to bear experiencing the child's feelings and one's own accompanying feelings until they have undergone

a process of internal modulation enabling the adult to make a
response in keeping with what the child has communicated, rather
than a reaction directed by the adult's own emotions.

These emotional reactions are likely to be very strong and,
whether we be therapists or substitute parents, we are liable to
find aroused in ourselves defences which are not dissimilar to
those of the deprived children. We require to be vigilant that our
receptivity is not being impaired by these defences and that we
too are not drawn into playing a part in the 'cycle of deprivation'
despite our firmest intentions to offer a relationship which provides
a path out of this cycle.

Full awareness of the child's loss and suffering is often nearly
as intolerable to us as it is to the child and, like the child, we
are tempted to use many ways of distancing ourselves from such
pain or to diminish the significance of loss, as in the following
two examples.

Betty, aged 8, last saw her mother when she was aged 2. Subsequently she had been fostered with her grandmother, then placed
in several children's homes and then with foster-parents. In her
assessment interview she made a rapid, shallow first approach.
Cheerfully she said, 'I always tell people that I have got no mummy
or daddy, then they feel sorry for me and give me lots of presents.'
The materialism, the exploitation of good will and sympathy and the
hint of incipient promiscuity are chilling; it is the other people
who are to feel sorry and perhaps guilty while Betty is carefree.
Yet this example may also reveal the way in which Betty has felt
that her own feelings of distress have not been attended to. Perhaps at an earlier time she sought a person who would be receptive
to the burden of her pain, who would hold her crying, but found
instead people who tried to cheer her up and divert her with gifts.
For such a child the most serious aspect of the deprivation may be
the deprivation of a person who can bear to allow the child to feel
her own feelings, who can contain the child's sadness and anger
and sense of having been cheated – and still be there tomorrow.

The second example concerns an adult, a woman in her thirties
who had been a professional housemother for many years. As the
time approached for her therapist to take a holiday she was amazed
to find that this aroused strong feelings of distress. Her mother
had died nearly two years previously, now her feelings about this
loss were rearoused and she wept painfully as she relived her
longing for her mother. When she had recovered a little she said
she had also been thinking about the children in her care, what
they must feel about losing their mothers. She added wonderingly,
'When the children left us, we never made anything much of it at
all. I'd wonder a bit how they would get on, but mostly I'd be
thinking of the next child who would be coming and hardly missed
the one who had left.'

Sometimes our response is not one of casualness, of diminishing
the significance of loss, but is rather one of anger; one wants to
blame someone for not having cared enough. Just reading the
child's case history may arouse furious indignation. It is only too

easy to see in retrospect the missed opportunities for adoption, for
supporting a fostering placement, for preventing rapid staff
changeover in a home and so forth. Engagement in the perplexities
of preventive work and a closer acquaintance with the strains on
the staffs of residential homes form useful checks upon my temptation to use anger as an easy way out.

When I convert my sense of pain into feelings of anger and blame,
I require to realise that I am myself behaving very like the more
anti-social of the deprived children. The pain which they cannot
endure to experience within themselves they tend to expel in ways
likely to hurt their caregivers.

As a therapist, one cannot allow oneself the comfort of passing
the blame on to someone else; in the child's eyes one stands for the
adult who is responsible for having failed him and one needs to be
ready to receive the child's outbursts of pain and anger if one is
ever to be able to help the child to bear with such feelings himself.

Feelings of anger are frequently apparent among the members of
the team concerned with the child. Therapists feel angry when
houseparents or social workers appear to be unreliable in supporting the regularity of the child's attendance at the clinic; when
lack of provision for escorts or transport thwarts the attempts to
establish therapy. And the social workers and houseparents feel
angry about the lack of support and appreciation from their
authorities or about the unreasonable demands of clinics and
therapists. The feelings of injustice, frustration and the wish to
blame someone seem to be endemic in this field of work. Although
such feelings may be partially appropriate, the anger becomes
disproportionate when it is also an expression of the ways in which
we are carrying the children's own angry feelings of having been
let down and the projection of our own guilt at being members of
the adult society which has allowed this to happen. When we come
to consider the individual child it becomes clear that feeling angry
on his behalf can play no appropriate part in facilitating a therapeutic relationship with him. It may even be harmful if the child
comes to realise that the adult is not containing anger but is passing it on to hurt others and is perhaps repeating a pattern of
quarrelling parents and family breakdown.

Both the anger at the supposed inadequacy of other caregivers
and also the intense compassion aroused by the child may lead to
a different response, especially when working with a child who has
been able to retain a yearning for parental care. The first clear
indication of this may be the therapist's discovery that he or she
has phantasies of fostering the child; the therapist's phantasies
of rescue, of providing for the child what all others have failed
to provide, match in with the child's phantasies of finding a long-
lost idealised parent. The child's fragile high hopes usually disrupt
painfully on the first occurrence of some minor frustration and his
subsequent antagonism and derisive rejection of the therapist are
likely effectively to demolish in the therapist any tendency to
self-idealisation. For a long period the child may continue to arouse
in the therapist feelings of inadequacy and guilt that he is 'only'

providing therapy. This experience can be used to help the child
to develop more realistic expectations and tolerance. Without such
preparation (see Chapter 10) the actual provision of fostering or
adoption may lead to a similar disillusionment for both child and
adult, when the child cannot forgive the substitute parent for not
being the incarnation of a phantasied idealised parent.

The contents of this book will have made evident the prevalence
of themes of rejection and counter-rejection, and emotional experiences of this nature are likely to be encountered again and again
by anyone who endeavours to enter into a therapeutic relationship
with a deprived child by developing receptivity to his communications. Very often these communications are not made in words or
even by means of the child's play; they are mainly to be discerned
in the feelings which the child, provocatively or subtly, arouses in
us. On being manifestly discarded by the child we may find ourselves feeling hopeless, useless, rebuffed, confused or downright
angry. Sometimes we find ourselves experiencing such feelings
while the child remains apparently more composed or indifferent,
more in charge of the situation, or detached, than we ourselves
can be. Once again there is temptation to give up, feeling so
belittled by the child it is easy to believe that he will not feel hurt
if one withdraws; more probably, it seems, he will feel indifferent
or possibly even relieved or triumphant.

The staff of children's homes are especially vulnerable to being
treated with contemptuous indifference. Like the therapists, they
are made to feel very fully what it is like to be ignored, despised,
helpless or even unreal and non-existent. Like the therapists
they feel themselves to be regarded by the children as the mere
rubbish collectors when the children feel themselves to be the
unwanted litter which must be kept off the streets. Soiling or messy
destruction of what is provided and insatiable demands for fresh
supplies can characterise the home as well as the therapy room.
The children's home staff may express this by perceiving themselves to be at 'the bottom of the pile' in the social services; they
share with the children the feelings of being neglected, deprived
of respect and rendered helplessly dependent upon 'the system'.
This makes them ready receptacles for the projection of the children's feelings of rejection. Unless supported to understand the
significance of such feelings as a projective form of communication
from the children, the staff are liable to react to their own hurt
feelings by leaving. By helping the staff to bear having a clear
look at the subtle complexities compounding their identification
with the underprivileged, we can both help them to deepen their
awareness of the child's feelings and also to obtain a more self-
respecting appreciation of the value of what their receptivity and
steadfastness can provide for the child. The alternative is likely
to be a rapid changeover of staff, followed by renewed demands
for fresh and increased supplies of houseparents to bear the burden; this yet again reinforces the trivialisation of relationships
and adds confirmation to the child's experience that feelings of
rejection are beyond toleration and can only be dealt with by

projection or flight.

What needs to be understood in such situations is not just that the child is perceiving the worker as the insufficiently caring parent of his past experience and revenging himself. Beyond this the child is also reversing the original situation; he is behaving towards the adult as he perceives himself to have been treated by his absent parents and is forcing the adult to suffer his insufferable feelings. This time the child feels himself to be the powerful persecutor and it is the adult who is the helpless victim. An examination of the manner in which the child inflicts pain and of the nature of the feelings of the recipient of the pain can reveal much concerning the individual child's particular internal experience of suffering. In such situations the adult cannot become genuinely trustworthy in the child's eyes until experience has shown that he has the strength to retain his own identity and value while simultaneously having the receptivity and empathy to enable him to experience and contain the projections of feelings that the child finds intolerable. It is often a long time before sufficient trust develops to enable the child to be aware of his dependency and needs and to dare risk approaching the adult with his longing for acceptance and affection.

Many of the children described in this book have behaved to their therapists with angry violence rather than with cold indifference. The therapist is then kept so busy trying to cope with physically dangerous and destructive attacks that it is extremely difficult to continue to function as a thinking person with the ability to reflect upon feelings rather than to react to them. The child seems determined to destroy the very capacity for caring attention and receptive understanding and to succeed either in making a fool of the therapist or in forcing him to become, like the child has become, an unthinking instrument of retaliation. The themes of rejection and counter-rejection have been sharpened to the cruel cutting edge of revenge and counter-revenge. This can take place when the child finds it impossible to contain within himself a state of internal torture and resorts to an externalisation of conflict. In this state the child both identifies with cruel, abusive figures and also attempts to provoke situations which will prove that the adults are as punitive and sadistic in external reality as they are experienced to be in the nightmares of his phantasies. To be caught up with a child in this state can be deeply disturbing to the therapist or substitute parent. Not only is the punitive, authoritarian role likely to be distasteful but also it is exceedingly alarming to realise that one's own sadism is being aroused.

The relationship may then be broken off not only because the worker is (with some reason) afraid of being the victim of the child's cruelty but, still more so, because he is afraid of his own feelings of violence towards the child. Exclusion of the child or the withdrawal of the adult is resorted to as the only apparent means of preventing an occurrence of abuse. A period of respite may enable the adult to face the arousal of his own sadism with less sense of shock and intimidation and thus to restore his ability to feel and think rather than to act. He may then be able to renew his contacts with the child with increased strength and be able to present the child with the possibilities of self-control rather than control by force and identification with the aggressor.

The therapist, like most caring adults, hopes to be able 'to be in touch' with the child's feelings. Painfully we learn that 'being in touch' is a torture for some children; what is intended to be a gentle approach to contact may be experienced by the child almost literally as a cruel stab at an open wound. Richard was a boy in our study whose attempt at therapy broke down after a few sessions. He not only broke off therapy in a very angry, rejecting way but, in the few months preceding and following this he was suspended from school several times because of his violence and eventually excluded. He rejected the offer of a holiday with a befriending couple - and then went to stay with them but behaved in such a way that they refused to have him back; he rejected several opportunities to visit his mother on Sundays and she pointedly failed to ask him again. He eagerly accepted the chance of having a home-tutor, but drove her away after a few weeks; he mysteriously acquired a lot of money and came before the courts; and finally he had to be sent away from his children's home as his violence was more than they could contain. Children such as these get caught up in such a violent spiralling sequence of rejection and counter-rejection that they seem compelled to continue until eventually prison is the only place willing to receive them.

With Richard there was a particular feature. His housemother reported that he could not bear to be touched. One occasion when he assaulted a teacher followed upon her touching him on the shoulder in a friendly way. It is possible that in his few therapy sessions he felt touched or in danger of becoming touched emotionally. A teenage girl who had spent most of her life in a children's home attended therapy with adequate regularity so long as she could maintain a defiant, anti-social and callous manner. She usually came in very thin clothing, clearly inadequate for the current weather, but she wore this with an air of bravado as though demonstrating that, unlike weaker creatures, she was tough and had no need of warmth. One day, however, she came with a pair of fur-lined gloves, borrowed from the kitchen cleaner, her only friend. She was unusually silent and spent most of the time fingering and tenderly caressing the fur. When I commented on this and her need for some warmth, tenderness and self-comfort, she looked at me with astonished alarm, shot off and never returned.

Such extreme vulnerability requires much sensitivity in the timing and wording of any approach and, for some children, one mistake may carry the threat of unbearable pain. As Donald Meltzer has said, sometimes one needs to 'tiptoe up to pain'. The injured child's capacity for feeling love and the need for love is so fraught with vulnerability that it is no wonder that his communications abound with images such as armoured vehicles, brick walls, ice walls or hedgehog spikes and snail's shells and similar means of warding off exposure to the pain of contact. Such children express their own attempts to make contact in terms such as fingers being pinched in doors and splinters jabbed into old grazes, and tears are only admitted as painful grit in the eye. A few children seem to perceive the very nature of contact in a relationship as being inevitably a matter of sadistic and perverse mutual mutilation. With these children sensitivity in modulating their pain goes hand in hand with much restraint and patience in modulating the offer of a possibility of being in touch with human warmth; the worker will ache with a longing to give while being obliged to recognise that compassion can only be received as though it were an attack.

It is apparent that the therapist, the foster-parent, the house-parent and the social worker (and also the reader of this book) have similar feelings in endeavouring to work and live with a severely deprived child. Experience of working with these children can aid the therapist to help other caregivers to tolerate and under-stand their painful feelings in providing for the children. The therapist needs also to realise that his contribution to the child is of a limited nature. The attention which he can give the child falls far short of substitute parenting. In one's own thinking one has to struggle to disentangle the certainty of the fact that the past is irreversible and the uncertainty of whether the damage caused is reparable or irreparable. Again and again the therapist and the child may together have to face the fact that the past cannot be 'put right'. Focusing upon the child's internalisation of experience leads to the complex view that the past is important only in so far as it continues to be alive within the child in his present life. We see this particularly in the emotions and phantasies which form the child's inner world and which impede his ability to respond to the present in a differentiated way, undisturbed by expectations derived from the past.

What the therapist can endeavour to do is to assist the child to become freer from the compulsion to repeat the past and thus to become more able to benefit from the relationships which others may make available to him in the present and future.

It is very painful for us to perceive suffering in children. We want to take action to remove the pain or at least to achieve a causative understanding which makes the pain more tolerable, more forgivable. But historical explanations can sometimes obscure the essentials rather than help us in our search for understand-ing. Often the simple truth is that our client, be it child or parent or substitute parent, is desperately unhappy, right here and now. It is this raw pain that requires our attention; it cannot be explained away, it has to be attended to and encountered in ourselves. We can never observe emotional injury; we can only observe the adaptations and maladaptations which each individual utilises in attempts to cope with pain. The pain remains unseen, our only perceptual organ for it is that most sensitive of instru-ments, our own capacity for emotional response. By maintaining our sensitivity without being overwhelmed or resorting to with-drawal or attribution of blame, we may then be better able to provide the answer which brings relief: the experience of a relationship with someone who can be relied upon to attend to suffering with both receptivity and strength.

GLOSSARY

Sheila Miller

ACTING OUT In psychoanalytic work with patients, intense feelings and impulses related to early anxieties and experiences are
aroused and are expressed in relation to the therapist. Emotions
aroused but not worked through in sessions can cause the patient
to behave outside the treatment room in a way which expresses
feelings which belong in the session.

'Acting out' in common usage sometimes refers only to wild
impulsive behaviour and this should be distinguished from the
sense in which it is used in this book.

BABY SELF In the therapeutic process of learning about conscious
and unconscious structures and processes it is possible and useful
to name parts of the self in order to describe precisely their level
of maturity and leading quality. The emotions and actions which
stem from, say, the 'baby self' can be distinguished from those
which relate to more mature levels of the personality, for example,
'little boy' or '10-year-old' self.

CONTAIN/CONTAINMENT In 'Learning from Experience' Bion
(1962, pp. 90-1) has used the model of a container and what is
contained to elucidate the process in which a baby projects overwhelming feelings into the mother who receives them, holds them
in her mind, and then conveys to the child the sense that the
anxieties are bearable and meaningful. The mother's ability to
'contain' will depend on a state of mind in which she is able to
take in the projections and to reflect on them - a capacity Bion
refers to as 'reverie'. After repeated experiences of this kind,
the process is internalised by the growing child who begins to be
more able to 'contain' his own anxieties; to follow the model, he
develops his own internal container. This can be conceptualised
as 'a space in the mind'. Containment is important in many other
relationships in addition to that of the mother and her infant.

The therapists whose work is described in this book all consider
that containment is of great importance in child psychotherapy.
Like the mother, the therapist must be able to tolerate the impact
of the doubts, anxieties, hostility and depression projected by
the patient; then to reflect on them and return them to the patient
in mitigated form.

COUNTER-TRANSFERENCE As used here the term refers to the
response of a therapist who is receptive to the transferred feelings
of the patient which can therefore be used in understanding the
patient's state of mind. In psychoanalytic writing counter-
transference often refers only to the therapist's inappropriate
responses to the patient, i.e. those which are connected with

the therapist's own private preoccupations and are not related to
the patient at all.

COUNTER-PHOBIC A person who adopts a counter-phobic attitude
to life is one who carries out, and takes pleasure in doing so,
precisely those activities which are felt to be dangerous and potentially anxiety-provoking. It is a form of manic defence whereby
anxiety is mastered by omnipotence, as if overcoming the fear by
seeming to deny the danger.

CARE/CHILDREN IN CARE In England, care provisions have been
designed to protect children whose parents cannot look after them
adequately. Children are taken into the care of a local authority
and the effect is to give the authority the powers and duties of a
parent or guardian. The social worker, acting for the authority,
decides what form of care is appropriate. This may involve residential placement in a foster-home, a children's home or a boarding
school. Occasionally children in care may live at home.

Children may come into care voluntarily with the agreement of
their parents, or compulsorily as the result of a court order.

DEPRIVATION Children are here described as 'deprived' when
they have not had adequate physical or psychological care or have
had neither. This might have commenced at birth or before or at
some later stage of their lives.

The term is used also to refer to deprivation which results from
the child's own internal processes, often resulting in a 'double
deprivation'.

Deprivation is thus used more broadly than by Winnicott (1966,
p. 6), who confined the meaning to the loss of good enough parenting already experienced, thus distinguishing it from 'privation'
by which he described a total lack of good experience.

INNER WORLD In the paper, Mourning and its Relation to Manic-
Depressive States, Melanie Klein (1940, p. 345) writes,

> Along with the child's relation first to his mother and soon to
> his father and other people, go processes of internalisation....
> The baby having incorporated his parents feels them to be live
> people inside his body in the concrete way in which deep uncon-
> scious phantasies are experienced - they are in his mind 'inter-
> nal' or 'inner' objects. Thus an inner world is being built up
> in the child's unconscious mind corresponding to his actual
> experiences and the impressions he gains from people and the
> external world and yet altered by his own phantasies and
> impulses. If it is a world of people predominantly at peace with
> each other and with the ego, inner harmony, security and
> integration ensue.

It follows that a disruptive world lacking in harmony and peace will
impede processes of integration.

MATERIAL Therapists refer to what is said and done by patients
in sessions as 'material'. This implies that what the patient says
and does is being interpreted in terms of latent as well as manifest
content. The 'material' would therefore always be regarded as a

communication from a person within a relationship and not only as
facts for inspection. Children communicate much of their conscious
and unconscious impulses and feelings through their play which
forms an important part of their 'material'.

OBJECT   This refers to 'that to which a subject relates' (Rycroft,
1968, p. 100). In psychoanalytic writings 'objects' nearly always
refer to persons, as in common usage one might say 'the object
of my affections'. This is in contrast to the use in developmental
psychology where objects denote things rather than persons.
In OBJECT RELATIONS THEORY the central tenet is the need of
the subject to relate to objects.
A distinction is made between external and internal objects, i.e.
persons who have been internalised; see INNER WORLD.

PHANTASY   Phantasies refer to the imaginative activity which
underlies all thought and feeling and are present and important
in every person throughout life. As used in psychoanalysis the
term essentially connotes unconscious mental content which may
or may not become conscious. English translators of Freud adopted
the spelling 'ph' in order to distinguish the predominantly or
entirely unconscious phantasy from 'fantasy' meaning daydreams,
etc. This meaning has assumed a growing significance, particularly
in consequence of the work of Melanie Klein on early development.
'Phantasy' is not regarded as something unreal in contrast to what
is actual, but as a part of the continuous living reality of the
inner world of the mind, i.e. psychic reality. The psychotherapist
can often observe emotions of which the patient is unaware and
from this information can infer what phantasies are present.
Pathological phantasies can be distinguished from normal phantasies
by the nature and degree of desire and anxiety associated with
them and the extent to which they affect or distort the experience
of external reality. In children's play their phantasies are acted
out and repeated clearly and dramatically with vivid detail. Interpretation of phantasies assists in working through and resolving
early conflicts and thus assists the patient to acquire self-knowl-
edge. The pathological content of phantasies can become modified
through psychotherapeutic work.

PROJECTION   The mechanism of attributing unwanted impulses or
emotions to someone else. This springs from the denial of experiences of mental pain or of guilty wishes. These are then felt to be
located in someone else.

PROJECTIVE IDENTIFICATION   The term was first used by
Mrs Klein in Notes on Some Schizoid Mechanisms (1946) to describe
the phantasy of projecting parts of the self or even the whole self
into the object. This results in an altered perception of identity:
the self might become identified with the object or the object might
be felt to acquire the characteristics of the part projected. The
recipient of such projective identifications will sometimes himself
experience the process as if he has in fact taken on the characteristics projected. These interchanges can take place in the context
of either normal and good relationships (as between mother and
infant) or pathological and hostile ones.

TRANSFERENCE   Freud (1905b, p. 116) observed that patients
repeat towards their analysts impulses and feelings experienced
earlier on in their relationships to people in their external lives.
He wrote that 'a whole series of psychological experiences are
revived, not as belonging to the past but as applying to the physi-
cian at the present moment....' Such repetitions, he found, made
it possible for earlier conflicts to be understood and thus to enable
psychological changes to take place in the patient. Melanie Klein's
work has extended the concept of transference to include the
transfer on to the analyst of the whole range of early emotions
as well as the projection of the infantile feeling states which persist
throughout life.

BIBLIOGRAPHY

Ainsworth, M.D.S. (1962), The Effects of Maternal Deprivation: A Review of Findings and Controversy in the Context of Research Strategy, in 'Deprivation of Maternal Care: A Reassessment of its Effects', Geneva, World Health Organisation Public Health papers, no. 14, p. 153.

Akins, F.R., Akins, D.L., and Mace, G.S. (1981), 'Parent-Child Separation: An Abstracted Bibliography', New York, IFI/Plenum.

Bentovim, A. (1977), First Steps towards a Systems Analysis of Severe Abuse to Children in the Family, 'Report of the Select Committee on Violence to Children'.

Bentovim, A., Jones, C.O., Lynch, M., McCarthy, B., Renvoize, J. and White, R. (1981), 'Child Sexual Abuse', Rochdale, British Association for the Study and Prevention of Child Abuse and Neglect.

Berse, P., (1980), Psychotherapy with Severely Deprived Children: Keith, 'Journal of Child Psychotherapy', vol. 6, pp. 49-55.

Bick, E. (1964), Notes on Infant Observation in Psychoanalytic Training, 'International Journal of Psychoanalysis', vol. 45, pt 4, pp. 558-66.

Bick, E. (1968), The Experience of the Skin in Early Object Relations, 'International Journal of Psychoanalysis', vol. 49, pt 2-3, pp. 484-6.

Bion, W.R. (1959), Attacks on Linking, 'International Journal of Psychoanalysis', vol. 40, pts 5-6, pp. 102-5, 90-1.

Bion, W.R. (1962), 'Learning from Experience', London, Heinemann, pp. 36, 90-1, pp. vii and x.

Bohman, M. and Sigvardsson, S. (1979), 'Longterm Effects of Early Institutional Care: A Prospective Longitudinal Study, 'Journal of Child Psychology and Psychiatry', vol. 20, no. 2, pp. 111-17.

Boston, M. (1967), Some Effects of External Circumstances on the Inner Experience of Two Child Patients, 'Journal of Child Psychotherapy', vol. 2, no. 1, pp. 28-32.

Boston, M. (1972), Psychotherapy with a Boy from a Children's Home, 'Journal of Child Psychotherapy', vol. 3, no. 2, pp. 53-67.

Boston, M. (1975), Recent Research in Developmental Psychology, 'Journal of Child Psychotherapy', vol. 4, no. 1, pp. 15-34.

Boston, M. and Daws, D. (eds), (1977), 'The Child Psychotherapist and Problems of Young People', London, Wildwood House.

Bowlby, J. (1951), 'Maternal Care and Mental Health', Geneva, World Health Organisation Monograph, no. 2, p. 12.

Box, S., Copley, B., Magagna, J. and Moustaki, E. (eds) (1981), 'Psychotherapy with Families: An Analytic Approach', London, Routledge & Kegan Paul.

Brazelton, J.B., Tronick, E., Adamson, L., Als, H. and Wise, S. (1975), Early Mother-Child Reciprocity, 'Parent-Infant Interaction', CIBA Symposium 33, Amsterdam, Association of Scientific Publishers, pp. 137-54.

Brill, K. and Thomas, R. (1965), 'Children in Homes', London, Gollancz, pp. 101-2.

Britton, R.S. (1977), Consultations in Child Care, (unpublished paper).

Britton, R.S. (1978), The Deprived Child, 'The Practitioner', vol. 221, September, pp. 373-8.

Chasseguet-Smirgel, J. (1978), Reflections on the Connections between Perversion and Sadism, 'International Journal of Psychoanalysis', vol. 59, pt 1, pp. 27-37.

Clarke, A.M. and Clarke, A.D.B. (1979), Early Experience: Its Limited Effect upon Later Development, in D. Shaffer and J. Dunn (eds), 'The First Year of Life', Chichester, Wiley, pp. 135-51.

Creighton, S.J. (1979), An Epidemiological Study of Child Abuse, 'Child Abuse and Neglect International Journal', vol. 3, no. 2, Oxford, Pergamon Press, pp. 601-7.

Dartington, T., Henry, G., Menzies Lyth, I. (1976), 'The Psychological Welfare of Young Children making Long Stays in Hospital', London, Tavistock Institute of Human Relations, CASR Document, no. 1200.

Dockar-Drysdale, B. (1968), 'Therapy in Child Care', London, Longmans, pp. 97-115.

Dockar-Drysdale, B. (1973), 'Consultation in Child Care', London, Longmans.

Fraiberg, S. (ed.) (1980), 'Clinical Studies in Infant Mental Health', London, Tavistock, pp. 164-236.

Freud, A. (1937), Identification with the Aggressor, in 'The Ego and the Mechanisms of Defence', London, Hogarth Press, pp. 117-31.

Freud, A. (1973), 'Beyond the Best Interests of the Child', New York, Free Press, p. 106.

Freud, A. (1976), Changes in Psychoanalytic Practice and Experience, 'International Journal of Psychoanalysis', vol. 57, no. 3, pp. 257-61.

Freud, S. (1905a), 'Three Essays on Sexuality', Standard Edition, vol. VII, London, Hogarth Press, p. 192.

Freud, S. (1905b), Fragment of an Analysis of a Case of Hysteria, Standard Edition, vol. VII, London, Hogarth Press, p. 116.

Freud, S. (1909), 'Analysis of a Phobia with a Five-year-old Boy', Standard Edition, vol. X, London, Hogarth Press, pp. 113-23.

Freud, S. (1916), Criminals from a Sense of Guilt, Standard Edition, vol. XIV, London, Hogarth Press, pp. 332-3.

Freud, S. (1923), 'The Ego and the Id', Standard Edition, vol. XIX, London, Hogarth Press, p. 26.

Freud, S. (1924), The Economic Problems of Masochism, 'The Ego and the Id', Standard Edition, vol. XIX, London, Hogarth Press, p. 155.

Freud, S. (1932), Anxiety and Instinctual Life, Standard Edition, vol. XXII, London, Hogarth Press, p. 106.

Furniss, A., Bridgman, K., Docherty, K. and Truckle, B. (1980), Jane and Mark Find a Family, in 'Adoption and Fostering', 102/4, pp. 34-42.

Giaretto, H. (1981), A Comprehensive Child Sexual Abuse Program, in Mrazek, P. Beezley and Kempe, C.H. (eds), 'Sexually Abused Children and their Families', Oxford, Pergamon Press, Chapter 14.

Hall, F., Pawlby, S.J. and Wolkind, S.N. (1979), Early Life Experiences and Later Mothering Behaviour: A Study of Mothers and their 20-week-old Babies, in D. Shaffer and J. Dunn (eds), 'The First Year of Life', Chichester, Wiley, pp. 153-74.

Harris, M. (1975), Some Notes on Maternal Containment in 'Good Enough' Mothering, 'Journal of Child Psychotherapy', vol. 4, no. 1, pp. 35-51.

Harris, M. (1976), Infantile Elements and Adult Strivings in Adolescent Sexuality, 'Journal of Child Psychotherapy', vol. 4, no. 2, pp. 29-43.

Henry, G. (1974), Doubly Deprived, 'Journal of Child Psychotherapy', vol. 4, no. 2, pp. 29-43.

Holmes, E. (1977), The Educational Needs of Children in Care, 'Concern', no. 26, pp. 22-5.

Holmes, E. (1980), Educational Intervention for Pre-school Children in Day or Residential Care, 'Therapeutic Education', vol. 8, no. 2, pp. 3-10.

Hoxter, S. (1977), Play and Communication, in M. Boston and D. Daws (eds), 'The Child Psychotherapist and Problems of Young People', London, Wildwood House, pp. 202-31.

Hunter, R.S. et al. (1978), Antecedents of Child Abuse and Neglect in Premature Infants: a Prospective Study in a Newborn Intensive Care Unit, 'Pediatrics', vol. 61, no. 4, April.

Hutten, J. (1977), Social Work Consultation to a Small Children's Home, in J. Hutten (ed.), 'Short-term Contracts in Social Work', London, Routledge & Kegan Paul, pp. 68-76.

Kafka, F. (1919), In the Penal Settlement, in 'Metamorphosis and Other Stories' (1961 edn), Harmondsworth, Penguin, pp. 167-200.

Kahan, B. (1979), 'Growing Up in Care', Oxford, Blackwell.

Kaplan, A. (1982), Growing Up in Foster Care: One Boy's Struggles, 'Journal of Child Psychotherapy', vol. 8, no. 1.

Kempe, R.S. and Kempe, C.H. (1978), 'Child Abuse', London, Fontana, pp. 61-3, 112.

Klein, M. (1932), 'The Psychoanalysis of Children', London, Hogarth Press, p. 29.

Klein, M. (1940), Mourning and its Relation to Manic-Depressive States, 'Contributions to Psychoanalysis', London, Hogarth Press, pp. 312, 345.

Klein, M. (1946), Notes on some Schizoid Mechanisms, 'The Writings of Melanie Klein', London, Hogarth Press, vol. III.

Klein, M. (1952), The Origins of Transference, 'The Writings of Melanie Klein', London, Hogarth Press, vol. III, p. 50.

Klein, M. (1957), 'Envy and Gratitude', London, Tavistock Publications.

Lambert, L., Essen, J. and Head, J. (1977), Variation in Behaviour Ratings of Children who have been in Care, 'Journal of Child Psychology and Psychiatry', vol. 18, no. 4, pp. 335-46.

Lozoff, B., Brittenham, M.D., Trause, M.A., Kennell, J.H. and Klaus, M.H. (1977), The Mother-Newborn Relationship: Limits of Adaptability, 'Journal of Paediatrics', vol. 91, no. 1, pp. 1-12.

Lynch, M. et al. (1975), Family Unit in a Children's Psychiatric Hospital, 'British Medical Journal', 2, pp. 127-30.

Martel, S. (ed.) (1981), 'Direct Work with Children', London, Bedford Square Press.

Meltzer, D. (1973), 'Sexual States of Mind', Perthshire, Clunie Press, pp. 87, 88, 105, 129, 130.

Meltzer, D. (1975), Adhesive Identification, 'Contemporary Psychoanalysis', vol. II, no. 3, pp. 289-303.

Meltzer, D., Bremner, J., Hoxter, S., Weddell, D. and Wittenberg, I. (1975), 'Explorations in Autism', Perthshire, Clunie Press.

Miller, L. (1980), Psychotherapy with Severely Deprived Children: Eileen, 'Journal of Child Psychotherapy', vol. 6, pp. 57-67.

Mrazek, P. Beezley and Kempe, C.H. (eds) (1981), 'Sexually Abused Children and their Families', Oxford, Pergamon Press.

Page, R. and Clarke, G.A. (1977), 'Who Cares? Young People in Care Speak Out', London, National Children's Bureau.

Polansky, N.A. (1981), 'Damaged Parents: An Anatomy of Child Neglect', Chicago, University of Chicago Press.

Pringle, M.K. (1974), 'The Needs of Children', London, Hutchinson, p. 135.

Reder, P. and Kraemar, S. (1980), Dynamic Aspects of Professional Collaboration in Child Guidance Referral, 'Journal of Adolescence', vol. 3, pp. 165-73.

Richards, E. (1971), Working with the Inner World of Children, 'Social Work Today', vol. 2, no. 15, pp. 5-8.

Rosenfeld, H. (1979), Difficulties in the Psychoanalytic Treatment of Borderline Patients, in J. LeBoir and A. Capponi (eds), 'Advances in the Psychotherapy of Borderline Patients', New York, Aronson, Chapter 4, pp. 187-206.

Rowe, J. and Lambert, L. (1973), 'Children Who Wait: A Study of Children Needing Substitute Families', London, Association of British Adoption Agencies.

Rutter, M. (1972), 'Maternal Deprivation Reassessed', Harmondsworth, Penguin.

Rycroft, C. (1968), 'A Critical Dictionary of Psychoanalysis', Harmondsworth, Penguin, p. 100.

Segal, H. (1973), 'Introduction to the Work of Melanie Klein', London, Hogarth Press.

Shengold, L. (1967), The Effects of Overstimulation: Rat People, 'International Journal of Psychoanalysis', vol. 48, pt 3, pp. 353-67.

Shengold, L. (1978), Kaspar Hauser and Soul Murder: A Study in Deprivation, 'International Review of Psychoanalysis', vol. 5, p. 457.

Social Science Research Council (1980), 'Children in Need of Care', Report of an Advisory Panel to the Research Initiatives Board, (Chairman, H.R. Schaffer), London, pp. 7-30.

Steele, B.F. and Alexander, H. (1981), Long term Effects of Sexual Abuse in Childhood, in Mrazek, P. Beezley and Kempe, C.H. (eds), 'Sexually Abused Children and their Families', Oxford, Pergamon Press.

Stoller, R. (1976), 'Perversion', Hassocks, Sussex, Harvester Press.

Szur, R. (1979), Psychotherapy with a Child who has been Poisoned, 'Child Abuse and Neglect', vol. 3, no. 2, pp. 505-9.

Szur, R. and Earnshaw, A. (1979), Experiences with Newborn and Very Young Infants, 'Nursing Times', 30 August, pp. 1497-1500.

Tizard, B. (1977), 'Adoption - A Second Chance', London, Open Books.

Tizard, B. (1979), Early Experience and Later Social Behaviour, in D. Shaffer and J. Dunn (eds), 'The First Year of Life', Chichester, Wiley, pp. 153-74.

Tod, R. (1968a), 'Children in Care', London, Longmans.

Tod, R. (1968b), 'Disturbed Children', London, Longmans.

Tod, R. (1971), 'Social Work in Foster Care: Collected Papers', London, Longmans.

Triseliotis, J. (ed.) (1980), 'New Developments in Foster Care and Adoption', London, Routledge & Kegan Paul.

Trowell, J. and Castle, R.L. (1981), Treating Abused Children, 'Child Abuse and Neglect', vol. 5, Oxford, Pergamon Press, pp. 187-92.

Tustin, F. (1960), unpublished communication.

Williams, A.H. (1976), Murderousness in Relation to Psychotic Breakdown, unpublished paper, p. 1.

Williams, A.H. (1980), The Indigestible Idea of Death, paper given at Diamond Jubilee Conference, Cassel Hospital, Ham Common.

Williams, J.M. (1961), Children who Break Down in Foster Homes, 'Journal of Child Psychology and Psychiatry', vol. 2, no. 1, pp. 5-20.

Winnicott, D. (1965), 'The Maturational Process and the Facilitating Environment', London, Hogarth Press and Institute of Psychoanalysis, p. 208.

Winnicott, D. (1966), Becoming Deprived as a Fact: A Psychotherapeutic Consultation,

'Journal of Child Psychotherapy', vol. 1, no. 4, pp. 5-12.

Winnicott, D. (1968), 'The Family and Individual Development', London, Tavistock, pp. 18, 132-145.

Wolkind, S.N. (1974), The Components of 'Affectionless Psychopathy' in Institutionalised Children, 'Journal of Child Psychology and Psychiatry', vol. 15, pp. 215-20.

Wolkind, S.N. (1977a), A Child's Relationships after Admission to Residential Care, 'Child Care, Health and Development', vol. 3, no. 5, pp. 357-62.

Wolkind, S.N. (1977b), Women who have been in Care: Psychological and Social Status during Pregnancy, 'Journal of Child Psychology and Psychiatry', vol. 18, no. 2, pp. 179-82.

Wolkind, S.N. (1978), Fostering the Disturbed Child, 'Journal of Child Psychology and Psychiatry', vol. 19, no. 4, pp. 393-7.

Wolkind, S.N. and Rutter, M. (1973), Children who have been in Care, 'Journal of Child Psychology and Psychiatry', vol. 14, no. 2, pp. 97-105.

Wolkind, S.N., Hall, F. and Pawlby, S. (1977), Individual Differences in Mothering Behaviour: A Combined Epidemiological and Observational Approach, in P.J. Graham (ed.), 'Epidemiological Approaches in Child Psychiatry', London, Academic Press, pp. 107-23.

INDEX